THE

INSTRUCTOR'S MANUAL:

OR

LECTURES ON SCHOOL-KEEPING.

BY S. R. HALL, A. M.

REVISED EDITION.

BOSTON:
PUBLISHED BY JOHN P. JEWETT AND COMPANY.
CLEVELAND, OHIO:
JEWETT, PROCTOR, AND WORTHINGTON.
1852.

ANDOVER: JOHN D. FLAGG,
STEREOTYPER AND PRINTER.

CONTENTS.

LECTURE III.

LECTURE IV.

LECTURE V.

LECTURE VI.

LECTURE VII.

LECTURE VIII.

LECTURE IX.

LECTURE X.

LECTURE XI.

LECTURE XII.

INTRODUCTORY REMARKS,

TO TEACHERS, AND CANDIDATES FOR THAT EMPLOYMENT.

YOUNG LADIES AND GENTLEMEN:

YOU have assumed, or expect soon to assume, the responsibilities of superintending the education of children and youth in the various schools demanding your services. As you direct your thoughts to that field of labor, nothing is more natural than an inquiry, What are the duties, what the trials and difficulties, what the pleasures and awards, of our vocation ?

In the following Lectures, it has been my purpose, in a very familiar manner, to discuss all these and kindred topics. Permit the remark here, that for what I attempt to impart to you, I am myself indebted principally to experience. When I entered the same field of labor, in 1816, there was scarcely a paragraph in the weekly newspaper, and not a single book or even *tract* within my knowledge, intended to aid the teacher, in knowing how to instruct and govern a school. Nor was there at that time a Teacher's Institute or Normal School within the United States, or even Europe. The magnificent school system of Prussia, which has since awakened such deep interest in Christendom, was not then matured. Though colleges, academies, and institutions for the training of men in the learned professions were long before established, it seemed to be taken for granted that those to whom was committed the training of children in the district schools, needed nothing more than a knowledge of the branches of study to be taught, in order to be qualified for their responsible duties.

I know not how other schoolmasters of that day regarded this fact, but to me it seemed a strange anomaly. Deeply sensible of my own want of suitable qualifications to train the young, as they should be, who were committed to my care, and believing that others were perhaps equally deficient, the inquiries were early suggested to my mind, What can be done to improve the qualifications of teachers, elevate the standard of common education, and increase the usefulness of schools generally? After considerable deliberation and correspondence on the subject, an institution was devised and established at Concord, Vt., in the spring of 1823, with the leading design, directly, to promote increased attention to the necessary qualifications of instructors, and indirectly to raise the standard of common school education, so far as the influence of that seminary might extend.

The interest awakened by these humble efforts of an obscure individual, during five or six years, and especially the interest manifested in the Lectures on the "Art of Teaching," the proper management and government of schools, etc., suggested the publication of Lectures on School-Keeping, for the benefit of primary teachers generally. These Lectures were first published in 1829, of which from fifteen to twenty thousand copies were circulated within a few years. In 1830, the Trustees of Phillips Academy in Andover, Mass., erected buildings for a Teacher's Seminary and Normal School in that place, and appointed the Author, as Principal. In conducting the exercises of that institution, and one of similar character, subsequently, at Plymouth, N. H., ample opportunity was furnished for a more full discussion and elucidation of the topics embraced in the Lectures on School-Keeping, previously published. A course of Lectures addressed to Female Teachers was prepared in 1833, intended to meet more appropriately the wants of that numerous and important class. Many publications by other authors soon followed, embodying the same leading thoughts, and, in some instances, embracing a wider range of topics. After an examination, however, of all these, the conviction in the mind of the author, is, that a volume embracing the leading thoughts of both the former publications, afforded at a price which is within the means of all, is still a desideratum, is hardly less needed than at any former time. The following Lectures embrace a part of those formerly published, and a part of those since prepared for his pupils, at the seminaries conducted by the author, at Andover, Mass., Plymouth, N. H., and Craftsbury, Vt. Also, extracts from lectures delivered before the American Institute of Instruction, in Boston, and before Teachers' Institutes in various places. In many instances, suggestions are made, and mere hints thrown out, where subjects would be discussed much more fully, were it not designed to make the price of the volume so small, that teachers of the most limited means can avail themselves of it.

The work is not only designed to be *studied* by the members of Normal Schools and Academies, who are candidates for the business of teaching, but to be carried into the school-house, as a guide in the performance of the *daily labors* there. That the work is perfect, or very nearly so, the author does not dare to hope; but he does believe that, if faithfully studied, and the spirit of the suggestions generally embraced and carried out, the labors of teachers will be made pleasanter to themselves, and result in conferring vastly increased benefit to the rising generation. Having devoted the best part of his life to the cause of popular education, the interest felt in it by the author is in no measure diminished with his increasing years, nor will it be, while he is able to employ his tongue or pen to advance it.

LECTURES ON SCHOOL-KEEPING.

LECTURE I.

YOUNG LADIES AND GENTLEMEN: —

THE vocation you have chosen is both highly honorable and important. To an extent greater perhaps than any fully apprehend, the progress of society and the destiny of the nation are in the hands of primary teachers. They have the moulding of the plastic material put in their hands, and all subsequent laborers can only modify their work. Next to the mother, the impress of the primary teacher is indelible. Were such what they should be, and did they know both *what* to do, and *how* to do it, the power *is* in their hands of moulding society at their will, and making it anything the benevolent, philanthropic, and Christian desire.

I fully embrace the sentiment of the late Dr. Channing of Boston: "I know not how society can be aided more than by the formation of a body of well qualified and efficient educators. We know not any class which would contribute so much to the stability of the state, and to domestic happiness. Much as we respect the ministry of the gospel, we believe it must yield in importance to the work of training the young. In truth, the ministry now accomplishes less, for want of that early intellectual and moral discipline by which alone a community can be prepared to distinguish truth from falsehood, to comprehend the instructions of the pulpit, to receive higher and broader views of duty, and to apply general principles to the diversified details of life. A body of cultivated men, devoted with their whole hearts to the improvement of education, and to the most effectual training of the young, would work a fundamental revolution in society. They would leaven the community with principles. Their influence would penetrate our families. Our domestic discipline would no longer be left to accident and impulse. What parent has not felt the need of this aid? has not been depressed, heartsick, under the consciousness of ignorance in the great work of swaying the youthful mind?"

Equally adapted to portray before you the nature of your vocation, is the language of another of the veterans in the cause of education:* "The word education, in its full extent, comprehends every influence exerted upon a person, from his first moment to the closing scene of life. Would you see a full exhibition of the power of these influences, go to yonder mansion, and look on the

* Rev. G. B. Perry.

child of yesterday. It has life, and the animal functions are going on; but knowledge to discern, or power to administer to its own wants, or even ability, with much distinctness, to make them known, it has not. Let the tender care of her who gave it birth be withdrawn a few short hours, and its connection with this world will come to a close, and its remembrance among men will perish. Hasten with it to the forest, and place it in the wigwam of the red man, and if it survives (which the hardiest alone can do) the severities which will meet it there, he will grow up erect and active, quick of sight, fond of the chase, and fonder still of war. Put him among the children of Ishmael, and he will become a wandering Arab, with his hand against every man, while every man's hand will be against him. Let him have his training in almost any part of the eastern continent, and he will be for caste, orders, and distinctions among men. Emperors and lords, and subjects and serfs, will in his ear sound like the ordinances of heaven. Let him dwell among us of New England, and he will acknowledge no distinctions but those of acquired worth; and no superiority but that which better actions confer. Put him among the *rich*, and he will need equipage and attendants. Put him among the poor, and those who will pay his hire may have his services. Class him with the middle orders of society, and he will be too independent to need a servant, and too noble himself to become one. Set him afloat in the world, and his particular attachment to place, to friends, and even his social feelings, will be lost. A sinking void will be experienced in his heart; he will live a wandering, joyless life, and at last go down to the earth without regret, and unregretted. Let him remain in the excellent family where heaven has given him birth, and his bosom will soon begin to heave with tenderness, and his heart to beat high at the pleasing sound of parent, brother, sister, friend. He will love his home; his mental and moral powers will open, and he will begin to multiply the comforts of that home, as well as to receive into his own bosom large portions of the varied happiness which there abounds. Carry him to the city of the Grand Sultan, and he will grow up a worshipper of Mohammed, and exhibit all the peculiarities of one of his most devoted sons. Let him live where the gospel sheds its benign and enlightening rays, and he will embrace the doctrines and rejoice in the precepts of Jesus.

"Such is the controlling influence which external circumstances must and will have upon all other children. And these external circumstances are nothing more or less than the concentrated influence, the whole education, through which a person passes, and by which he will be benefited or injured, in proportion to the healthful or baneful nature of the sum of this influence. Of what unspeakable importance, then, must it be to this heir of life and immortality, that this influence should be enlightening, elevating, and moral; that he be under the influence of virtuous associates, judicious parents, and truly intelligent, virtuous, and patriotic teachers.

"The rising generation, like clay in the hand of the potter, are readily moulded into almost any shape, and will certainly take the form, adopt the principles, and fall into the habits which the all-fashioning power of education — comprehending under that term whatever in the world around operates on the mind or heart — shall give them. Of the direct and overwhelming interest which all have in this subject, it is not easy to imagine, much less to speak. The whole future condition of the rising generations, in all their mental, social, and moral interests, their present and future joys and sorrows, is involved in it. Even those of us who are now on the stage, are scarcely less interested in it; for in a few years more, if alive, we must be thrown upon them for every enlightened and kind attention which the debilities of growing age will make necessary and comforting to us. Nor will it stop with us. It reaches forward to generations still to come, whose mental acquirements, whose social feelings, whose moral principles, whose religious institutions, literary advantages, and civil rights, to a very important extent, must be handed down by those who came before them.

"On a subject whose influence is so deep, wide, and stirring, it is not possible we should feel too absorbing an interest, or direct our thoughts and inquiries too frequently to it. And I cannot help considering it among the most encouraging circumstances of the present day, that there has been called up so general and operative attention to this subject.

"Among the causes which operate with such

fearful power upon human character and human conduct, school-education holds a *highly interesting and important place.* The period of life in which childıen are at school, the time they pass there, the employments which occupy their attention, the associations into which they are brought, the sentiments which are inculcated, and the control exercised over them, with many other circumstances, more or less obvious, all concur to give the school-education a most important bearing upon their future lives and prospects."

The educator and instructor of children, is, in the language of the law, *in loco parentis*, in the place of the parent; and if so, as many are intrusted to his care, he assumes the responsibility of many parents in one.

It has been well said, "every family is a little republic;" and it may with the same propriety be added, every school is a little kingdom, and from these is made up the great state, or nation. These schools, established in this land by Puritan wisdom, are the glory of our land, from which every male member, as he comes up to maturity, steps into the great copartnership of the nation, and becomes part of the government thereof.

You are to become the cultivators of a soil,* on

* "A child, like a plant, grows up and expands and blossoms, and bears fruit, according as it shall be guided, nourished, pruned, and guarded by those to whose care it is submitted. Its little eye is ever open to behold, and its ear quick to hear, and its heart ready to receive impressions, which every act and word of those who are around cannot fail to make in all that they perform or say in its observing presence. I venture to assert that there is not one in this assembly, who, if he will

which, as *yet*, has been sown little seed; and which, if preoccupied before the fowls of heaven have scattered that which is noxious, we may hope will yield desirable fruits. You are to watch, and water, and nourish plants, which are not to remain always in the nursery; they must soon be removed to other fields, where their growth and expansion will very nearly correspond to the early culture they have received.

You will therefore indulge me in directing your attention to the high importance of the labors you are to perform, and to the results which must unavoidably follow.

They are *young*, it is true; but each revolving sun adds to their age. They are ignorant, perhaps, but they have noble powers and capacities for development. They see every object around them; and they notice whatever is uttered in their hearing. *They are young*, but so was Alexander, once; so were Bonaparte and Washington. The "mad boy," whom the monarch of Persia sent his satraps "to seize, and bind, and scourge," was, twenty years before, in his cradle, or on his mother's knee. The conqueror of Italy had hardly

---

reflect but a little upon his past existence, cannot recur to habits which may have cost him many a tear, and which originated in some casual circumstance of childhood. Some thoughtless act, sanctioned by the praise and example of a parent, guardian, or instructor, may lay the foundation of future happiness or misery in the mind of the child who is beholding him; and when that parent, or guardian, or instructor shall have ceased to exist, there may be immortal minds still on the earth, for whose actions he shall be at least partly accountable, because they proceed from principles which were instilled by his example, and perhaps nourished by his care."—*Rev. Dr. Blagden.*

numbered the years of manhood, when the trump of fame announced him "the hero of the age," and crowned heads trembled before him. A very few years were sufficient to mature their gigantic minds.

The group of children before you are both young and ignorant. And who of all the busy multitude around you were not equally so, a little time since? The Hottentot and the savage may, in manhood and in age, continue *children* in knowledge; but for those who have commenced their existence in a republic renowned for knowledge and patriotism, there *ought* to be, there *will* be, another destiny. These children must acquire knowledge, either proper or improper, beneficial or injurious. They will form characters, good or bad. Instead, therefore, of presenting a reason why your attention to the children before you is unimportant, their *age* presents one of the strongest reasons why you should feel the *deepest* interest in them, and bestow on them your most assiduous attention.

The effect of habits formed in childhood will be as lasting as life. If these habits are such as it is desirable they should be, numerous evils will be averted, and important good secured; but if a wrong bias is given in infancy, or childhood, obliquity must be expected in every subsequent period. Experience demonstratively proves, that "a child left to himself bringeth his mother to shame." Children are often more ready to form wrong habits than right ones. The experience of this led the Psalmist to say, that they "go astray as soon as they are born."

Will you tell me, these are things which belong to parents, and have no claims on you? That you are to teach them the first principles of science, but have no farther duty to perform? Before suffering yourselves to rest on this ground, let me ask you to reflect seriously on several things.

First, what is the character and situation of many parents? They *ought* certainly to be most tenderly alive to the best interests of their offspring. They ought to be well acquainted with the dangers to which children are exposed, and the best means of averting them. It ought to be their daily and hourly care, to "train" the beloved beings of whose existence they have been instrumental in "the way they should go."

But what *are* the facts? Is it true that even a majority of parents, especially of those whose children attend the free schools of the State, appreciate parental responsibility? Many parents seem to have no thought beyond the necessary provision for the temporal wants of their children. Many send their children "to school to learn manners" and *morals*, as well as letters, which they never attempt to teach them at home. Others furnish their offspring with constant examples of everything that is unlovely and revolting. Look at that mother, surrounded by her numerous offspring. Her husband is perhaps intemperate, or engaged in labors which require his constant absence from home. She must therefore control them when in health, and attend to their incessant calls; must administer to them in sickness, and, in fine, perform all that is done for them. Is it not nearly *impossible* for her to govern, train, and instruct them in the best way? But if it were possible, what does she know or realize of the nature and importance of her duty? She was perhaps a servant before marriage, or belonged to a family situated like her own; or, perhaps, was deprived of all opportunity for instruction on the nature of parental duties, before she became a parent. And could she be expected to make those advances in knowledge afterwards, which are necessary for the station she occupies?

I have presented a case strongly marked. But there are many such instances, and some in almost every district. Many mothers are dependent on their daily labor for sustenance. Others are found, whose thirst for gain is so great, that their children are *secondary* objects of solicitude.

These children will soon arrive at manhood, and become active in the community. They, if sons, will be freemen, and must exert an influence on others. Many of them, in turn, will become parents. All of them have commenced an existence never to terminate. And let me beg of you to remember, that all the salutary influence which will be exerted upon many of them, will be limited to that which they will feel in the district school. Let them grow up unrestrained in their passions, unintelligent and immoral, and their influence must be destructive to the peace, morals, and happiness of society, as well as their own.

Another consideration which adds interest to

the office sustained by you is the *unbounded influence* which you can exert over your pupils. The *kind and affectionate teacher* is, in the estimation of the child, the standard of truth and excellence. What the teacher approves must be right, and everything disapproved must be wrong. Here, then, a power is put into your hands, which renders your office one of peculiar interest and importance. You are responsible for the use you make of it. If you cultivate a habit of discrimination, the same habit may be easily formed in those who are under your instruction; and on this habit in them will depend the justness of their conclusions on many subjects connected with their present and future welfare.

The child who reasons correctly on *one* subject, will be led more easily to reason correctly on others. Teach him to entertain just views of his duty to his instructors, and you will easily lead his mind to perceive the nature of the duties he owes to his parents. Lead him to reason right with regard to the treatment of his school-fellows, and he will at once be prepared to perceive the higher claims his brothers and sisters have upon him. The teachers who lead their pupils to cultivate kind and affectionate feelings towards each other, not only send a happy influence into every family from which the school is collected, but also transmit this influence to future generations. *Young* children are capable of appreciating things where their happiness is affected; and this impression is not easily destroyed when they advance to maturer age.

The confidence which your juvenile charge repose in you, puts their destiny, in an important degree, into your hands; and must tend, I think, to excite in your bosoms feelings of deep interest towards them. So far as you desire to promote happiness and prevent misery, to remove ignorance and disseminate knowledge, to purify society and elevate human character, so far you must be interested in your employment, and in those waiting to drink in instruction from your lips. It is easy to bend the pliant twig. So the *earliest* impression made on the mind and heart of childhood usually remains the longest, and shapes the character of manhood. The *age* of your pupils, therefore, presents one of the strongest inducements to great faithfulness in cultivating everything lovely, and checking the growth of everything noxious and unlovely, in character. Let me repeat it again; the *age* of the group of children before you, presents a high claim to your *most faithful and untiring efforts to do them good.*

It is your work to take these children as you find them, and to train them with reference to their duties as citizens of a free country, as members of society, and as moral agents, under the government of the great Creator.

LECTURE II.

YOUNG LADIES AND GENTLEMEN: —

HAVING made several suggestions in the preceding Lecture, with regard to the nature of the employment you have chosen, it may be proper here to advert to several *evils you will experience, and difficulties you will encounter*, in securing the highest beneficial results from your efforts.

While there are some honorable exceptions, it is still obvious to every discriminating observer, that, from primary or district schools generally, there is not that degree of benefit there ought to be. The members of these schools are not generally as *well educated* as the safety and happiness of themselves or the interests of society demand.

While I am not prepared to indorse the declaration made by a foreign committee of examination, that the "school system of the United States is an utter failure," and that "not one scholar leaves these schools qualified for the duties of a citizen and a man," I *am* constrained to believe that common schools do fall vastly short of that degree of usefulness which is desirable, is attainable, and which ought to be expected. Various things tend to this result, to which your attention should be directed, as a means of removing difficulties or surmounting obstacles.

In the various fields you will be called upon to cultivate, you will no doubt detect, and be forced to mourn over, apathy and indifference, with regard to primary schools. There is generally, perhaps, no want of conviction that education is important. Very few are found, even among the ignorant, who are slow to acknowledge that learning is necessary to usefulness and enjoyment. Among the well educated, no remark is more frequently heard, than that a good education is necessary for every citizen in a land of civil and religious freedom. But it is equally obvious to me, that, while the importance of education is generally acknowledged, the *immense value of common schools* is not realized. When it is recollected that from these minor fountains of knowledge, and from these only, the great mass of the community receive all their instruction, the marked indifference to their character and usefulness which so often appears is truly astonishing.

This indifference has as many phases as the chameleon has colors. In one district, it is developed by the meagre attendance at the school-meeting; where three, five, or ten only, out of twenty, thirty, or fifty voters, are all who are habitually present. In another, by the appointment of a committee, to act for the district in procuring a teacher and superintending the interests of the school, totally unfit for the office, having neither the knowledge necessary to judge of the qualifications of a teacher, nor to estimate the qualities of a good school. In some neighborhoods, indifference is exhibited by suffering an old and dilapidated school-house to stand year after year, — cold, dark, untidy, and uncomfortable, — in which, were parents obliged to sit, for a day or a week, they would regard it as an intolerable burden; at least, many seldom *dare* to make trial of it for an hour.* It is a matter for rejoicing that this indifference is declining, and has diminished essentially within a few years. But it has not diminished to that degree which would justify me in omitting to mention it as a great obstruction to the usefulness of schools. A want of *parental supervision* and watchfulness is another of the evils you will meet, if not everywhere, at least too generally. Parents seem to repose a degree of confidence in the instructors employed, which they repose in no other class of laborers. What farmer would employ a young man of twenty years of age to take care of his cattle at the barn, and neglect to visit his barn for the season? What merchant would employ a clerk, and fail, for three months, to make any examination of the state of the books kept by him, or of the business he transacted? What housewife would intrust the care of her dairy to "hired help," and neglect for three months to enter her dairy-room and examine the state of it?

* An exact description of some of the school-houses the author has examined within a few years, would, if given, be scarcely credited by a portion of the community. It would really seem as if they were contrivances for papal torture, and intended for making pupils "perfect through suffering." Such are even now sometimes found in thriving villages, by the side of the elegant church, the comfortable academy, and the tidy and commodious dwelling-house.

Facts like the following are of too frequent occurrence. Mr. ——, of ——— county, owns two hundred sheep, which are usually kept on a farm four miles from his house. He employs a very faithful man in the neighborhood to feed them during the winter, but goes regularly *twice a week* to look at them, and examine the "state of his flock." In a school-house, half a mile from his dwelling, he has six children, who have been placed under the care of three or four different teachers; and yet for several years he has not once visited that school, to examine the state of "this other flock."

From statistics collected with care, it has been ascertained that less than a twentieth part of the parents in a county, have visited the schools attended by their children, once a year. This want of parental supervision is not confined to one county or State, but is almost universal.

Among the many other obstacles to success in your labors, the irregularity of attendance on the part of scholars is not the least. From the statistics collected in many parts of the country, during several years, it is shown that about one-third part of the scholars of suitable age, lose the benefit of public schools almost entirely. In many districts, lateness of attendance is a very serious evil. Multiplicity of books,— multiplicity of branches of study, the defective character of many of the text-books used,— and in some instances a great deficiency of books, will be found evils of no ordinary magnitude.

The negligence of parents to furnish apparatus for the purposes of illustration of the studies pursued in common schools, is an evil *very* general. Most of our school-houses are as naked as the walls of a prison; neither maps, globes, nor other articles being furnished; and in many, not even a blackboard sufficiently large to be of any real value. Neither books for general reference, nor libraries are provided, except in one or two States, for the benefit of district schools. An appropriation of a few dollars annually, in every district, for these objects, would be far more valuable to schools, even if this were taken from the amount raised for the payment of instructors, than if appropriated in any other way.

To some evils of another character, also, I wish to advert. There are few school-districts where there is not, from some cause or other, a disagreement among parents, that eventually grows into a "party thing." This has originated, often, from causes at first very trifling, and has been in some instances continued from father to son. Sometimes difference of religious opinions has caused it. Sometimes parties have arisen from different political views. At other times, merely the location of the school-house, or of the families that compose the district, has originated difficulties and divisions that have been kept up for many years. One part of the district is more wealthy than another, or more enlightened; or a part of the families may be connected with each other by consanguinity, and combine to form a party, and in this way strife is engendered. There is sometimes a party that wishes great severity in school, and another that wishes laxness of government. One party is in favor of having an instructor from *college*, and another wishes one who has never been in sight of it; one party wishes to give high wages, and another cares only for an instructor who will keep "cheap." A thousand trifling causes give rise to these ever-varying divisions, and, go where you will, you may be told of the "Congregational party," the "Baptist party," the "Presbyterian," or "Methodist," or "Universalist," or some other party, formed by disagreement in religious opinions. You will be told of the "Democratic party," the "Federal party," the "Administration party," or some other, growing out of political disagreement. You will be told of the "hill party," the "meadow party," the "river party," the "school-house party," etc., etc. Now the influence of all these party divisions and feelings, is to diminish the usefulness of the school. Happy would it be if these things were confined to parents; but children imbibe the same feelings, which are carried to the school and cause dissension there.

Another source of injury to common schools, is the disposition of the more wealthy to place their children at some academy or high school. Many are able to bear the expense of sending their children to some seminary of higher order, and hence feel but little interest in the common school. Its character is a subject of little interest to them. A few unsuccessful efforts to have the school what they wish end in discouragement, and they often say, "Well, if we can't have a good school at home, we *can* send to the academy." Such institutions are now so common, that there is little difficulty in doing it. It is certainly a subject of great importance to the success of elementary institutions, that the wealthy and intelligent should strive to increase their usefulness and elevate their character. By withdrawing their influence and assistance, the work is left to those who have not the means and character to afford the requisite support.

I wish here to allude to another cause, which has an influence in preventing the usefulness of primary schools. It is an evil of a negative character. There is a want of Christian effort to raise the standard of moral influence in schools. The impulse of Christian enterprise, at the present day, has led to associations for benevolent effort on almost every subject except this. We hear it mentioned as a cause for lamentation and regret, by Christians and clergymen of every denomination, that common schools are so often seminaries of vice. It is a remark which has often fallen on my ear, that "our children learn more evil than good; increase in vice faster than they gain in knowledge." Indeed, so general is this feeling in many places, that Christian parents are accustomed to say, when any new vicious habit is discovered in a child, "He learned it at school." Is it not surprising, that, with these facts so prominent, no combined effort among professed Christians has been exerted on this subject? Is it one on which effort would be hopeless? Is there no ground to believe, that exertion on the part of Christians, would be successful in elevating the moral character of our schools? I know that *individuals* have acted right. Individual districts have used their best efforts to obtain moral instructors. But this is by no means sufficient. "*Union is strength.*" United and persevering effort is needed on this, as well as on other subjects with which the happiness of society is so intimately connected; and deserves attention, if the *literary* improvement of the young is alone regarded. The most orderly, the most moral school, will make the best progress in study. Moral motives are the best inducements to a faithful improvement of time. It may always be expected by committees of visitation, to find the most subordination, the best progress in learning, and the most correct deportment, where the greatest interest has been awakened in regard to the moral character of the school. I will not undertake to say, that every effort of combined Christian influence would be productive of the effect desired. But it does seem to me just, to attribute a portion of the defect in the usefulness of schools to a want of such effort and influence.

The things already mentioned are all hinderances to the usefulness of schools, and some of them are evils of great magnitude. Resulting as they do, from a great variety of causes, some of them may be expected in nearly every district. And instructors should regard themselves very fortunate who do not encounter more than one. But I should do injustice to my strong convictions, should I neglect to call your attention to another, which I must regard not only greater than any one, but greater than all, to which I have called your attention. It is one, too, in which you are more deeply implicated than in all others.

The great reason why schools do not result in unspeakably greater good to the rising generation, is the INADEQUATE QUALIFICATIONS OF TEACHERS.

While this is true, I do not wish to imply that the blame is *solely* or *chiefly* chargeable on the members of your profession. When, in succeeding Lectures, I state what are the essential qualifications of a good teacher, I think you will fully accord with me, in regarding the inadequate qualifications of instructors as involving others in blame quite as much or more than yourselves. In order to secure adequate qualifications to the members of our profession, means must be provided greatly in advance of those which have been furnished in our country, or any other except Prussia. True, and I greatly rejoice in it, "a juster estimate of the teacher's profession begins to prevail," and some feeble efforts have been put forth to provide for their training.

Normal schools have been commenced in a few

places within the last quarter of a century; and Institutes of a few days' or a few weeks' continuance, are provided for by the legislatures of several States, or individual benevolence; and a few books have been written with special reference to the wants of this class of laborers. But even now, in this age of enterprise and improvement, in the latter half of the nineteenth century, there is not, on the western continent, one seminary established and endowed for the purpose of educating teachers, where they can enjoy facilities for this purpose equal to those provided for students in law, medicine, or theology. It is by no means strange, that, when the facilities for the appropriate training of teachers are so imperfect, they do not, as a class, possess higher qualifications. Indeed, it is rather matter for wonder, that so many have attained eminence in the profession, and that we can refer to such names, among our females, as Read, Grant, Lyon, Hasseltine, and Beecher; and among the other sex, to those equally honored as the benefactors of their race. But the remark of Channing, made twenty years ago, with regard to those placed at the head of primary schools, is, if not universally still too generally true: "It seems generally to be thought that any body may become a teacher. The most moderate ability is thought to be competent to the most important profession in society. They who squander thousands on dress, furniture, and amusements, think it hard to pay comparatively small sums to the instructor; and through this ruinous economy, and this ignorance of the teacher's vocation, they rob their children of the aid for which the treasures of worlds can afford no adequate compensation." "There is no office," he adds, "higher than that of a teacher of youth; for there is nothing on earth so precious as the mind, soul, and character of the child. No office should be regarded with greater respect. The first minds in the community should be encouraged to assume it. Parents, should do all but impoverish themselves, to induce such to become the guardians and guides of their children. To this good, all their show and luxury should be sacrificed. Here they should be lavish, while they straighten themselves in everything else. They should wear the cheapest clothes, and live on the plainest food, if they can in no other way secure to their families the best instruction. They should have no anxiety to accumulate property for their children, provided they can place them under influences which will awaken their faculties, inspire them with high and pure principles, and fit them to bear a manly, useful, and honorable part in the world. No language can express the cruelty or folly of that economy which, to leave a fortune to a child, starves his intellect and impoverishes his heart. There should be no economy in education. Money should never be weighed against the soul of a child. It should be poured out like water for the child's moral and intellectual life.

"Parents should seek an educator for their children who will become to them an hearty and efficient friend, counsellor, coadjutor in their work. If their circumstances will allow it, they should so limit the school, that the instructor may know intimately each child, may become the friend of each, and may converse with them frequently in regard to each. He should be worthy of their confidence, should find their doors always open, should be among their most welcome guests, and should study with them the discipline which the peculiarities of each pupil may require. He should give the parents warning of the least obliquity of mind which he discovers at school, should receive in return their suggestions as to the injudiciousness of his own method in regard to one and another child, and should concert with them the means of arresting every evil at its first manifestation. Such is the teacher we need, and his value cannot be paid in gold. A man of distinguished ability and virtue, whose mind should be concentrated in the work of training as many children as he can thoroughly understand and guide, would shed a light on the path of parents for which they often sigh, and would give an impulse to the young, little comprehended under our present modes of teaching. No profession should receive so liberal a remuneration. We need not say how far the community fall short of this estimate of the teacher's office. Very many send their children to school, and seldom or never see the instructor, who is operating daily and deeply on their minds and characters. With a blind confidence, perhaps they do not ask how that work is advancing on which the dearest interests of the family depend. Perhaps they put the children under the daily control of one with whom they do not care to associate. Perhaps, were they told what they ought to pay for teaching, they would stare as if a project for robbing them were on foot, or would suspect the sanity of the friend who should cause them to throw away so much money in purchasing that cheapest of all articles, that drug in every market,— instruction for their children."

On any other subject of equal importance, spirit-stirring appeals would be made from one end of the land to the other. A remedy would be speedily sought, found, and applied. But in reference to *this* subject, what has been *done?* What has been *attempted?* Hundreds of thousands of children are every year committed to the care of teachers very unfit for their work, at the imminent hazard, it is manifest, of all parents and patriots hold precious in our civil and religious institutions.

I speak of a state of things which ought to excite the surprise and astonishment of every reflecting mind.* Where shall we look for an

* "Our entire system of common school education needs to be placed on a higher and more liberal foundation. Our youth can never be well and competently instructed in our schools as they now are; and these schools can never be what they ought to be, to meet the wants of the community, till the compensation for teaching be raised far above what it now is; till, indeed, it be such as to exalt teaching to a profession, and make it an object for persons of talented minds and high qualifications, to choose it as their calling for life. This, in my opinion, is the great desideratum which needs to be realized in our land."—*Rev. Dr. Hawes.*

4

explanation, which will justify it? Is there anything peculiar in the institutions transmitted to us by our fathers, which will account for it? It will not be pretended. Shall we refer it to the existing government and laws of the country? It is impossible. Is it because the people of this country are so *selfish*, so *calculating* in their views, that they neglect thus the interests of their children? How wretched the economy, which, to amass for them a fortune, "starves the intellect, impoverishes the heart!" We boast of our intelligence. Can it be, that an intelligent people will long be indifferent respecting the character of those who are to make the rising generation *intelligent?* Is it a mark of intelligence, to educate men for every art and profession, except that of training the mind and forming the habits of the young? Our fathers have bequeathed us a rich legacy in providing, at much expense of blood and treasure, the happy form of government under which we live. But who does not know that the pillars which support it are the virtue and intelligence of the people? We cease to be a *free* people, the moment we cease to be a *well-instructed*, *virtuous* people. Is this peculiarity of our civil condition a reason why we should be indifferent respecting the means of education? No. It suggests a motive certainly for attention to the subject, which no man who loves his country can consistently disregard.

We look in vain, however, for adequate reasons to justify the indifference which has been so prevalent, in regard to the character of teachers. Obvious as it is, upon the slightest reflection, not only that their standard of qualifications should be immeasurably elevated, but that their number should be at this moment more than doubled, it is still a deplorable fact that no well-digested plans have yet been proposed and *executed*, adequate to secure either of these important results. There would be less occasion to wonder at this, if the people of the United States were in the habit of showing similar apathy in reference to other enterprises, even those of inferior importance to that of which I am speaking. But what say facts on this point? A canal is needed from the Hudson to the lakes. Can it be made? is the first inquiry. The unhesitating answer is, Yes! And the call for millions of capital, which accompanies it, is responded to as soon as it is made. The money is furnished; and the next step which remains is immediately taken; — the work is *begun* and *finished*. It is represented that railroads, connecting Boston with Lowell, Worcester, Providence, Portland, Albany, Burlington, Rochester, New York, and Montreal, will be of great public utility. True, hills of granite must be broken through, valleys must be filled up, rivers must be crossed, and a thousand obstacles surmounted. But the enterprises are practicable, — are commenced and completed. Engineers, laborers, and funds are found without difficulty. Take another example: A monument, perpetuating the achievements of Bunker Hill, is due, it is thought, to the fathers of the Revolution, from their happy, grateful descendants. What money is needed for the purpose ? is asked. Half a million of dollars is no obstacle in the way. Let it be erected, and we will provide the sum, ten thousand citizens instantly respond.

It is not with any design of censuring them, that I allude to facts of this nature. I rejoice that canals can be dug, railroads constructed, and monumental columns reared,—

"To tell of glories past, and deeds of war."

It is well these things *should* be done. They are honorable witnesses to our enterprise, and thrift, and public spirit. But who will assume the responsibility of making the assertion, that our varied applications of the steam-power, our railroads and canals, will add half as much to our security, happiness, or even wealth, as that *course of education* which would make our children *industrious, intelligent, and virtuous ;* which would result in securing to them health of body and mind, and which aims also to fit them for the service of Him, who is the rightful proprietor of all.

And what has yet been done for accomplishing these results? True, we have schools of high merit, where the powers of the intellect are cultivated. Our colleges and professional seminaries are ornaments as well as blessings to the land. Many men have been educated in them, who have done honor to the country, and benefited the world. We have also hospitals for the sick, schools for the deaf and blind, asylums for those deprived of reason, and a multitude of *practical schools* for teaching and learning the trades and arts of life. But where is the *educator* to find that adequate instruction so essential to his success in the arduous employment of guiding the footsteps of the young in the paths of virtue and knowledge ?

It is not thought that a man is qualified to offer his services in the healing art till he has been under the care of learned lecturers, who, by description and demonstration, can illustrate the thousand "ills that flesh is heir to," and make him acquainted with the various modes of treating the diseases of the body. But where are learned lecturers employed in making the future instructors of our youth familiar with the character and mode of treating the more dangerous diseases of the intellect and the heart.

The fault in question is justly chargeable, in part, to parents and others ; but not wholly. The elevation in the qualifications of instructors, during the last ten or fifteen years, has not been so rapid as the improvement in the means. These means, I admit, are far, very far, below what they ought to be ; but they are vastly greater than they were thirty years ago. Can it be said that instructors are as much better qualified now, generally, as the means for it have been augmented ? I think every one, who can compare that period with the present, will be forced to come to the conclusion that such is not the fact. So that after all the blame that may justly be attributed to parents, a large share rests on teachers themselves. When the Legislature has made appropriations for Teacher's Institutes, to be held in a given county, or has established a Normal school for the State, what proportion of those who instruct schools in that county or State avail themselves of the proffered advantages ? It would be easy to show that not more than a fourth part of the instructors engaged in teaching in a county are usually found at the county Institute, where such are established. A proportion still less are found to avail themselves of the advantages of the Normal school, where established. A most valuable library for every teacher is provided in the lectures delivered before the American Institute of Instruction, costing less than a dozen dollars. How many common school instructors own that library ? In how many academies is it found ? Some of these lectures are worth their weight in gold, to any teacher. So far as the means for your improvement are furnished, and you fail to improve them, the evils resulting from that neglect are justly chargeable to yourselves. Allow me, in closing this Lecture, to use the language of another.*

"If I were asked, what is wanted in our country to secure the perpetuity of its institutions, and to promote, in the highest degree, the prosperity and happiness of the people ; I would answer : not mothers only, but teachers, well qualified and

* Dr. Hawes's Lecture before the American Institute, 1845.

faithful teachers of youth, dispersed through the land, and liberally and honorably sustained in their office. Sure I am, that it will never be well with our country till this most important *desideratum* is realized; and whoever contributes, even in the humblest measure, in the attainment of so great a result, deserves to be honored as a friend of his country and a benefactor of his race."

LECTURE III.

YOUNG LADIES AND GENTLEMEN: —

IN connection with the closing suggestions of the last Lecture, I propose in this and the following one to discuss the *requisite qualifications and duties of instructors*. I connect these subjects, because in several respects the duties to be performed very naturally suggest the qualifications necessary. To these subjects it may be expected you will be disposed to direct attention specially in order to decide whether duty calls you to enter or continue in this field of labor; as no one can expect *success* in an employment for which he has not the requisite *essential* qualifications.

Instructors, in common with those in other professions, should possess all the ordinary faculties of body and mind. They need to exercise all the senses, and all the faculties of body, common to our race. It is however true, that the loss of sight in one, and the loss of hearing in another, the loss of a hand or foot, have not prevented *in dividuals* from becoming highly useful teachers. Deficiency in one respect, has awakened greater interest in others, and thus a measure of compensation has been secured. The common faculties of mind are still more essential. One deficient in reason, memory, judgment, imagination, taste, conscience, etc., cannot hope to succeed well in a vocation requiring the exercise of all these faculties in himself, and requiring the due training of them in others.

Several things may be *first* spoken of, which will inevitably prevent a desirable measure of success in teaching.

1. Ignorance of its responsibilities, must present an insuperable barrier to usefulness and success.

The station of any one intrusted with the care of children is immeasurably important. No one can have intercourse with them for an hour, without making an impression on them which may last during life. This is particularly true of those who are required to control, govern, and instruct young minds, for a considerable period of time. The taste, the temper, the disposition, the thoughts, and habits may all be influenced and made to incline in almost any direction the teacher may choose. And if one occupying a station so important has not an impressive sense of responsibility, I know not how success *can* be expected. But there is another important view of this subject. Where responsibility is not realized, *effort is generally feeble.* It is commonly true, that he who realizes *most fully* the responsibility attached to his calling, will be found the most efficient and untiring in his labors. It is certainly natural to anticipate faithful effort in any one whose views of the character of his employment are distinct and elevated. And I must believe, that any one who contemplates the calling of a teacher as devoid of high responsibility and of peculiar importance, has no right to hope for success.

2. A want of *interest in the society of children* will inevitably unfit one for the labors of teaching, governing, and interesting them.

There are those who apparently contemplate a company of children with about the same feelings that they would a company of *apes*, whose mischievous pranks are to be the source of constant vexation and complaint. Others would consider life as most highly fraught with ills, if it must be spent in the presence of those whose elasticity and buoyancy are such as prevent them from being classed with mutes and dolts. And how can such persons gain the confidence or secure the love of children? Yet without these, you have an uninviting company to guide and control. A child will ascertain in an hour the character of your feelings towards him, and whenever you betray a disrelish for his society, you cannot readily induce him to obey you with cheerfulness and exactness. "Love is the loan for love." You may have all the various knowledge of a learned professor, may be profoundly versed in the mysteries of science, may drink deeply from the fountains of literature, but if you do not *love children*, you are unfit to be their teachers; for they will not, they cannot, and I may say they *ought* not to love you.

3. Ignorance of the manner in which children imbibe ideas, must prevent success in teaching them.

Here, I am disposed to believe, is one of the prominent reasons why so many fail in their attempts to communicate instruction. To those accustomed to trace the operations of their own minds only, there is a strong inclination to suppose that what is intelligible to themselves is intelligible to children. I have not unfrequently heard teachers, when giving instruction to a class of young scholars, use language far better adapted to the college lecture-room than to the place of primary education. "It is so perfectly plain that any one can understand it;" yes, it *may be very plain to you*, but very far from being so to your scholars. Would you not believe a person intended to insult you, who should show you the various parts of a complicated machine, and explain them only in the technical language of his profession, and then expect you to understand it as well as he, after years of labor and study?

Teachers, who suppose that the young are able to think in the same way, and acquire ideas in the same manner, they do, after a long course of mental discipline, have yet to take the very first steps in a course of preparation for their work. Children learn by induction; and it is not to be expected of them, that they can analyze, till the mind has been trained to such an exercise. If you are to teach children, *you must know how children think*. To know this, look back and remember how *you* thought, how *you* reasoned and formed conclusions, when you were children. If unable to do this by the aid of your own memory, learn it from your intercourse with children, and by watching the operations of their minds, while instruction is imparted to them in such a way as to make it intelligible. Many opportunities of this kind will occur, which should be improved with the highest care. Let me press this point still more. To say nothing of the loss of time consequent from your ignorance of its importance, the disrelish which your scholars may form for study will be very injurious. The difficulties which arise from rendering a study unintelligible become associated with the study itself, and not unfrequently the little learner sits down in despair of ever being able to accomplish his task. The repugnance which many show to the study of arithmetic or grammar, is generally the result of an unskilful course of instruction pursued by teachers. A professional gentleman of high respectability remarked, not long since, he never understood arithmetic, till he heard his little son repeat and explain his exercises in Colburn's "First Lessons." And he added, that this was owing to the manner in which he was directed to study it when he was a school-boy ; at which time he acquired so strong a distaste for it, that he could never overcome it in his subsequent course. Hundreds of similar instances have passed under my observation, and I have no doubt others may be furnished by your own recollection.

4. Ignorance of human nature, especially of the peculiar characteristics of children, unfits any one for becoming their instructor.

There are chords which, if touched, will vibrate in harmonious unison, and others which never fail of producing discord. If there is manifest ignorance of this fact, it cannot be expected that harmony and improvement can be secured by the labors of such an instructor. Children are not all alike. They have been governed differently, if governed at all, and are diverse in their dispositions and temper. One is amiable, and another the reverse ; one has learned submission to necessary laws, and another must be made to learn it. One can understand you, while another is seemingly incapable of it. If you are unacquainted with these facts, or are so unfortunate as to suppose that the same manner is to be adopted with all, you can hardly fail of injuring some. Almost the same variety of character is to be met with in primary schools as is found in a more extensive community. The only difference is, there the *bud* or *early blossom* is seen; in this, the fruit has grown and ripened.

It is not only important to understand *these*

different and various shades of character, but also to know those principles of human nature which are nearly uniform in all. There is a way to reach the sympathies of every individual. Acquaintance with this throws the person almost completely in your power. If actuated by a benevolent desire to do good to your interesting charge, you may, by this key, enter the arena of every heart, and establish your empire over every mind. Without this, it is impossible for you to succeed to the satisfaction of yourselves or others. You must know how to influence children, if you wish to benefit them to the extent of your power.

5. Those to whom the labor of teaching is irksome, and who enjoy no pleasure in observing the opening powers of juvenile minds, I would advise never to assume the responsibilities of *teachers*.

Before a person who is engaged in any occupation in which he is uninterested, there can be only a dreary path. His task is a heavy and painful one. His exertions will be feeble, and his hopes of success must be limited. To one of high moral feeling, the sense of duty *may* be sufficient to induce *constancy and faithfulness* in labor. But I am unable to believe that in any case, under these circumstances, the *same* success is realized, which may be rationally expected where the employment itself is a source of constant enjoyment. It is unreasonable to expect it.

It may be asked, do not all take pleasure in the exhibition of opening intellect? and can *any one* fail of being pleased with a situation favorable for observing it? Admit the truth of this; still, there is a wide difference between merely *witnessing* results, and active employment in *producing* them. It gratifies me when I see the operations of some interesting machinery, but it does not follow that I must be pleased with the employment of making it. Nor does it follow that, because I am delighted with observing the progress of some grand design, I should be found in possession of those traits which would give me pleasure in executing it. There are those who appear to take pleasure in many things which cost them no serious effort, but who are the last to be gratified by the same things when obliged to be the agents in their accomplishment. Many are ready to declaim in favor of the interesting business of the instructor, who would be the last to delight in the labor of it themselves. But if there is not pleasure in the labors involved in the office, success must, to say the least, be doubtful.

6. *Impatience* must be a barrier to success in teaching.

In training the young mind, "line upon line," and "precept upon precept," are indispensable. The forwardness of one, and the ignorance of another; the confidence of some, and the diffidence of others, are to be met. If the thousand little unpleasant occurrences of the day are sufficient to prevent you from preserving that evenness of temper which is desirable, you are not prepared to make your labors pleasant to yourselves or agreeable to your scholars. Impatience throws a shade over every object. It discolors everything with its own medium. When under its influence, time drags heavily. Obliged to wait an hour longer than you expected, to meet a friend, no other society can make amends for the disappointment.

For those who instruct children, a large share of patience is indispensable. Unless *scholars* can be preserved from impatience, there must be an end to quiet submission to authority and cheerful attention to instruction. Impatience is a contagious disease. It can never be the disorder of *one* without exposing *others* to its direful influence. If you are impatient, you must expect others to contract the distemper. No one can envy your situation, if impatient yourself and surrounded with others equally so.

Having just adverted to several things which must prevent, I proceed to state distinctly several things requisite to, success in teaching. Some of these it will be seen are nearly opposite to some already mentioned.

1. Among these, *common sense* is indispensable. No teacher can succeed well without it. Do you inquire, *what is common sense?* It is not very easy to define it accurately, but I mean by the term, that faculty by which things are seen or apprehended as they are. It implies a proper appreciation of the properties of life, and guides to judicious plans of action, under the varied circumstances in which persons are placed. It implies good judgment and discretion; it is the exer-

cise of reason uninfluenced by passion, prepossession, or prejudice. It is nearly the same in *men*, as *instinct* in *brutes*. Then again, common sense is not genius nor talent, as commonly defined, but better than either. It is not a meteor, dazzling with its rays for a moment, but a constant and shining light. Some have great powers of mind, and yet are deficient in *common* sense. They speak, think, act, or judge, differently from the great mass of the community. One may be very amiable, and may have strong desires to do good, and yet fail of success in any office or employment, for want of common sense. Common sense will lead one to act, under all circumstances, in that manner which will be approved by the community in general, after due opportunity to perceive the bearings of an action.

2. *Uniformity of temper*. Where this is wanting, it is hardly possible to govern or teach with success. He whose temper is constantly varying, can never be uniform in his estimation of things. Objects change in their appearance as his passions change. What appears right in any given hour, may appear wrong in the next. What appears desirable to-day, may be regarded the reverse to-morrow. An uneven temper must, in any situation of life, subject one to many inconveniences. But when placed in a situation where his every action is observed, and where his authority must be in constant exercise, the man who labors under this malady is especially unfortunate. It is impossible for him to gain and preserve respect among

his pupils. No one, who comes under the control of a person of uneven temper, can know what to expect or how to act.

3. A capacity to *understand and discriminate character*. The dispositions of children are so various, the treatment and government of parents so dissimilar, that the most diversified modes of governing and teaching need to be employed. The instructor who is not able to discriminate, but considers all alike, and treats all alike, does injury to many. The least expression of disapprobation to one, is often more than the severest reproof to another; a word of encouragement will be sufficient to excite attention in some, while others require to be urged by every motive that can be placed before them. All the varying shades of disposition and capacity should be quickly learned by the instructor, that he may benefit all, and do injustice to none. Without this, well-meant efforts may prove hurtful, because ill-directed, and the desired object may be defeated by the very means used to obtain it.

4. It is desirable that teachers should possess much *decision of character*. In every situation of life this is important, but in none more so than in that of which I am treating. The little world by which they are surrounded is a miniature of the greater. Children have their aversions and partialities; their hopes and fears; their plans, schemes, propensities, and desires, as much as older persons. These are often in collision with each other, and not unfrequently in collision with the

laws of the school, and in opposition to their own best interest. Amidst all these, the instructor should be able to pursue a uniform course. He ought not to be swayed from what he considers right. If he be easily led from his purpose, or induced to vary from established rules, his school must soon become a scene of disorder. Without decision, the teacher loses the confidence and respect of his pupils. I would not say that, if convinced of having committed an error, or of having given a wrong decision, you should persist in the wrong. But I would say, that it should be known as one of your first principles in school-keeping, that what is required must be complied with, in every case, unless cause can be shown why the rule ought, in a given instance, to be dispensed with. If you have given a hasty or unreasonable decision, frankly confess it.

5. Teachers ought to be *affectionate.* The human heart is so constituted, that it cannot resist the influence of kindness. When affectionate intercourse is the offspring of those kind feelings which arise from true benevolence, it will have an influence on all around. It leads to ease in behavior, and genuine politeness of manners. It is especially desirable in those who are surrounded by the young. Affectionate parents usually see their children exhibit similar feelings. Instructors who cultivate this trait, will generally excite the same in their scholars. No object is more important than to gain their love and good-will. In no way is this more easily accomplished than

by a kind interest manifested in their welfare, an interest which is exhibited by *actions* as well as *words*. This cannot fail of being attended with desirable results.

6. Capacity to exercise *just moral discernment*, is indispensable. They who teach, are no less under *law* than they who are taught. They are accountable to themselves, their employers, the State, and society in general, and to God. If they seem to have no appreciation of this, how can they cultivate a sense of moral obligation in their pupils? If they violate the rules of decorum, the regulations of good society, the laws of the State, or the commandments of Jehovah, how can they expect to cultivate in children obedience to the same rules, or to the regulations and laws of the school? As the happiness or misery of men results more from what they do or neglect to do, than from what they know or do not know of literature and science; as virtue more certainly promotes safety and happiness than knowledge; as the virtuous will be happy, though deficient in science, and the vicious man must be miserable, how much soever he may know, teachers are under the most weighty obligation to train the young to virtuous habits, by example, as well as precept. The remark of an ancient philosopher, that "boys ought to be taught that which they will most need to practise when they come to be men," is most true. To cultivate virtuous habits, and fix virtuous principles; to excite a sense of duty to God, and of dependence on him, should

be the first object of teachers. If they permit scholars to indulge in vicious habits; if they regard nothing as sin, but that which is a transgression of the laws of the school; if they suffer lying, profaneness, and other crimes, to pass unnoticed and unpunished, they are doing an injury for which they can in no way make amends. An instructor without moral feeling, not only may ruin the children placed under his care, but does injury to their parents, to the neighborhood, to the town, and doubtless to other generations. The moral character of instructors should be considered a subject of very high importance; and let all, who *know themselves to be immoral*, renounce at once the thought of such an employment, while they continue to disregard the laws of God, and the happiness of their fellow-men. Genuine piety is highly desirable in every one intrusted with the care and instruction of the young; but morality, at least, should be *required*, in every candidate for that important office. He cannot teach others to do *right*, while he does that which is wrong in their presence, — to obey the laws of Jehovah, while he openly violates them; and with a friend* I entirely coincide, who remarks: —

"The daily life should be one of strict purity and propriety. No moral blemish on the external character can be tolerated, in one to whom is committed, as to the teacher, the formation of the character of the young. And this correctness of

* Rev. N. Munroe.

the outward deportment should be well secured by correct and long-cherished moral habits. Nor is even this enough. It should spring from right moral principles; be the fruit of a mind and heart in love with moral excellence and beauty.

"The teacher needs to be deeply convinced of the reality and immutability of moral obligation; of the divine sanctions which attend and sustain a moral government over the world; that man is an accountable being; and that between virtue and vice, as also between virtuous and vicious conduct, there is a distinction which the Almighty Governor of the universe will never overlook nor disregard.

"Here is a point on which it is all-important that the teachers of our youth should be sound. Their views of crime, of sin, of moral beauty and deformity, should be correct, as well as their constant practice. And the more fully this is the case with any company of teachers, the greater, I cannot doubt, will be their success in governing and training their pupils."

LECTURE IV.

YOUNG LADIES AND GENTLEMEN: —

1. AMONG other essential qualifications, instructors should be able to understand *the diversities of character* of their pupils. Among pupils there

will be great diversity. Some will love learning, and desire to make all the improvement of which they are capable; others will have no taste for learning, and no desire to be improved. Some will be easily governed; others will require all your wisdom, firmness, and prudence, to restrain them from what is wrong, and lead them in a better course. Some have formed habits of application, and others have been brought up in idleness. Some will be too bashful; others, too bold. Some will be benevolent and affectionate; others, selfish and unsocial. Some will be found very nearly what you desire them to be; others, the opposite in everything. Such are the diversities that will be found in every school.

With regard to two extremes, teachers are exceedingly liable to misjudge; these are, precocity and uncommon dullness. Precocity in a child very generally gives high pleasure both to the parent and teacher. But it should be known to every teacher, that such as develop this, require peculiar treatment. Precocious children are liable to great danger, and are not unfrequently ruined, or nearly so, by those powers which to those around, if not to themselves, become subjects of so much interest.

If a child can acquire knowledge with surprising facility, it is exceedingly dangerous to urge him to that effort by which the brain is exercised at the expense of other parts of the body. Such a child needs the most careful physical training, or his nervous system may become deranged, and his health lastingly impaired. Many such children find an early grave, resulting from the ignorance of parents, or the injudiciousness of teachers. Others have been made invalids for life; and though possessed, perhaps, of fine powers of mind, are unable to put forth any effort answerable to the expectations formed. Some become permanently diseased in mind, and suffer partial or permanent derangement. A more common form of precocity is that of an unusual power of memory. If this be cultivated at the expense of other faculties, the result must be an unbalanced mind. Great power of memory may be developed, where there is deficiency in judgment, in the power of comparison, or in ability to digest the facts acquired by memory, so as to make them of real worth. If the teacher fail to know this, he is in danger of misapprehending the greatest necessities of his pupils. To praise a child for the attainment he makes, perhaps with very little effort, tends to inflate him with vanity, "that *wen* of the mind, which deforms and hinders its growth." He is often thus led to neglect the effort essential to ultimate success. "The natural gifts of mind are bestowed on none so abundantly as to supersede the necessity of continued mental exertion." But it does often happen, that the "wonderful *child*," being no longer a *child*, is no longer a wonder. The powers that were wondorful then, by perversion or neglect, are in manhood almost or entirely lost. Overtax the powers of a child during childhood, and you inevitably produce premature decay.

But the instructor needs equally to be able to apprehend the origin of uncommon dullness. "There is," a good writer has observed, "a remarkable variety in the growth of the mind, from the first visible dawning of reason to the full maturity of its powers. Of minds that finally arrive at an uncommon degree of intelligence, some have a slow growth; an ample harvest of fruit succeeds to no ordinary blossom. Neither their childhood nor their youth gave promise of the powers of mind developed in manhood." Unusual dulness, is almost always disagreeable to an instructor. But it should be known, that such dulness is by no means the certain precursor of insignificance. The dullest child may become an intellectual giant. A child may be at six, eight, or ten years of age, utterly unable to retain a single idea when he attempts to recite it, or to comprehend a rule perfectly plain to another, of that age, and yet this furnish no proof of a *weak* mind, or of want of effort on his part. Of one who became the president of one of our most renowned colleges, it has been said, he could not learn to read till he was eight or nine years old. Dr. Scott, the author of a Commentary on the Bible, could not compose a theme when twelve years old, to whom, even much later, it was matter for wonder that any one should ever have ideas enough to write a folio volume. Even later than this age, Dr. Adam Clarke could not, as he informs us, after incredible effort, commit to memory a poem of a few stanzas only. At nine years of age, one who afterwards became a chief-justice, in this country, was, during a whole winter, unable to commit to memory the little poem, found in one of our school-books, " You'd scarce expect one of my age," etc. Yet these individuals developed powers of mind in manhood seldom surpassed.

Two instances within my own sphere, of similar character, have been observed, and many others less strongly marked. I would never despair of any one, however slow his progress, that is not stubborn, — that makes effort, and that has capacity to learn other things. The dull should be encouraged, instead of being rebuked or punished, and such methods adopted, as will be most likely to lead them to make effort. It is excessive cruelty to make such the butt of ridicule, on account of their tedious progress.

8. Instructors ought to be sufficiently acquainted with the laws of health, to be able to guard those under their charge from the dangers to which they are liable while at school. These dangers are numerous, several of which I ought, perhaps, to specify *particularly*. One, and a most common one, is the breathing of impure air in a school-room without proper means for ventilation. If a house be small and close, and the school large, this danger is daily experienced. Another danger, and one very common, arises from an attempt to secure ventilation during the time scholars are *in the house*, by opening windows, doors, etc., by which they are exposed to a strong current of cold air while the body is heated. Drop-

ping the upper part of a window is more dangerous, than raising the lower, because the cold air falls directly upon the heads of those exposed to it. The German rule, "Never sit in a current of air between two doors or windows," if universally observed would save much suffering from colds, and other diseases resulting therefrom.

Another danger, from which serious evils result to scholars, is that of sitting in school *with wet feet*, or *damp clothes.* To females, especially, this practice is exceedingly injurious, and no teacher who understands the danger will permit it. Many have found an early grave from such exposure.

Another danger results from exercise so violent as to induce profuse perspiration during recess, and then sitting in a cold part of the school-room without putting on additional clothing. The dangers to scholars from these and other sources, should be known by every one placed at the head of a school, or evils may be experienced by scholars both lasting and painful. Ignorance on these subjects disqualifies any one for the office of instructor. Many, already, have been the costly sacrifices to such ignorance. I will take time here to advert to only one other physiological danger, that of too long-continued confinement. A distinguished physician observes: "Many facts lead us to doubt the wisdom of keeping children, large or small, confined for so many hours in school, and confined as they are generally on seats, or at desks, where the body and limbs are cramped for want of room. A little boy who loves his book, said to his father, in my presence, 'Father, I always wish, when at school, that the four hours could go off in one, — because my back and legs ache so, sitting.' What physiologist does not sympathize with the poor child who has to bear, in this age of activity and motion, confinement which would be intolerable to any parent or school-master? What is more likely to render learning a toil, and to give the school-room the character of a place of penance? Any position or confinement which renders the body uncomfortable, acts as a dead weight on the mind, and subtracts from it a proportionate amount of power, and retards intellectual progress.

"Six hours daily confinement on hard and uncomfortable seats, to very young children, indeed, to most under twelve years of age, is a cruelty to which no parent, though much better able to bear it, would submit. In childhood and early youth, it is more important to secure the healthy exercise of all the organs of the body, and to lay the foundation for good health, than to secure the attainment of any given amount of knowledge." All the arrangements of the school-room should be made, as far as possible, with regard to this object.

9. Another qualification essential to success, is *ability to govern.* This is indispensable. Those who cannot govern, should never offer themselves as candidates for the teacher's office; for if you fail on this point, every endowment of nature,

every attainment by study or experience, will be unavailing. An ungoverned, disorderly school, is a sad spectacle to every friend of youthful improvement. Without an ability to *govern well*, it is impossible to *teach well.* If the stubbornness of one, and the waywardness of another, cannot be subdued; if children cannot be reduced to order and submission, you can do nothing for them which will materially conduce to their benefit. Fail not to remember this remark, day by day. By ability to govern, I do not mean simply a capacity to awe children into submission to your wishes by fear of punishment. This may secure attention to your orders while the scholars are seated before you, but cannot produce that regularity and uniformity which are essential to their improvement. By ability to govern, I do not wish to be understood to approve of that powér, which some possess, of making every one fear being in their presence. It is said of the Gothic invaders of Italy, that the glance of their eye was sufficient to dishearten the boldest Roman soldiers. A haughty sternness may terrify, will repel, but cannot soothe, attract, and charm. A severe and angry look may excite fear and aversion; but it cannot secure confidence and affection.

Firmness, discretion, and kindness combined, are the principal requisites in forming the character of a good disciplinarian. Firmness, in pursuing a proper object; discretion, in granting or denying the requests; and kind feelings towards the subjects of government, must always be united in those who exercise authority, if they would render their office pleasant to themselves, or salutary to others. Visit the school of A, and you will find the strictest order and quiet without apparent effort. Every pupil is under the influence of an irresistible charm, and seems to have no inclination to do wrong. Visit the school of B, and you will think every child is a savage. The latter teacher scolds, complains, and punishes, from day to day, and lives in bedlam still; the former merely waives a hand or casts a look upon the school, and all is order, all is peace. The whole secret of the difference in the two cases is this, one knows how to *govern;* the other, only how to *punish.*

The importance of this subject will be more fully seen by the following considerations: Judicious government is essential to *progress* in study. "Order is heaven's first law," stamped on the very face of nature. It would be unphilosophical, therefore, to expect great intellectual acquisitions where there *is not* order. This can be established only where some suitable *penalty* is attached to its violation.

Government implies law; and if laws exist, the right to enforce them must exist also. Where no such right is delegated to teachers, it is impossible to render instructions valuable. The human mind is so constituted, that without long training it cannot avoid giving attention to the objects around, and of course cannot practise sufficient abstraction to study in the midst of confusion and misrule.

Calm, continued, and patient attention to the principles of science, and the application of these principles, is requisite to enable pupils to retain a knowledge of them. It is obviously impossible for any one to give such attention where his rights are not secured. On such security no one can depend, where no penalty is attached to the violation of law.

School government is indispensable in order to secure the *great objects of education.* I use education here in its broadest sense. These objects are, to develop all the faculties of the mind, invigorate the senses, cultivate and guide the affections, govern the passions, and lead the young to act under the moral sanctions of their being. Or, in other words, the great object of education is to fit the young for duty, safety, usefulness, and happiness in all the periods of their existence.

Without discipline, which of these ends can be secured ? We have seen that positive acquisition cannot be made in the midst of disorder. Disorder must prevail where discipline is *not* maintained. It must be impossible, also, to expand and strengthen the powers of the mind; as this can be done only by calling them into vigorous exercise, and strengthening them by use. The memory, taste, judgment, imagination, are all to be cultivated in order to the proper improvement of the intellect; but which of these faculties can be trained where a school is a place of misrule and a scene of disorder? Can the memory be improved in the midst of interruption? Can the taste be cultivated in the midst of irregularity? the judgment rendered accurate and acute from examples only of its abuse? And as for imagination, how far it can be accurately educated, in such circumstances, I need not stop to inquire.

I said, it is one of the objects of education to cultivate the kind and social affections. From the proper exercise of these much of the happiness of life results. But in a school without discipline, they must find a soil more sterile than the Nubian desert, blasts colder than the winds of Greenland, and vapors more destructive than the breath of the sirocco. And yet, what is man without a heart, without affections? What is man, when he makes himself the centre of the universe? What is man,—unsocial, sordid, misanthropic,—but a libel on himself, as he came from the hands of his Maker?

The child, who is never taught to bow to any law but that of self-will; to submit to no restraint but positive necessity; to regard no right but his own, is equally unfitted to possess or communicate enjoyment. While at school he is in the midst of a miniature world, and if he is not led to cherish kind and sympathetic emotions towards those around him, he will, of course, be left to cherish feelings of an opposite character.

But this is not all. A school not brought under proper discipline is often the hot-bed of the *evil passions*. Anger, revenge, malevolence, selfishness, develop a most vigorous growth, and too often attain a gigantic strength. The school, then, devoid of order, law, and submission, does not merely fail of accomplishing the positive good that is intended, but does lay the foundation for great and lasting evils, both to its members and society. Here indeed are taken, perhaps, the first regular lessons in nullification, and are formed the first resolves to set at defiance the laws of society and of Jehovah. Let me illustrate by an example: "I didn't mind her, and she can't make me do it," said a little urchin, as he fled from the school-house after having broken the hold of his teacher; "I didn't mind her, and I never will mind another teacher as long as I live." The teacher exclaimed, "Well, I am glad you are gone." How many such lessons have been taken in our schools, intrusted to inefficient teachers, or in the family of inefficient parents, another day will fully disclose. That they are frequent, the confessions of criminals too fully show.

A habit of cheerfully submitting to the laws under which we are placed by our Creator is, obviously, of the highest value. Without it, happiness and safety are out of the question.

I shall recur to the subject again, in another Lecture, on the general management of schools; and will only add in this place, that inability to govern a school you must regard as an absolute disqualification for the teacher's vocation. And if you have just ground to fear failure here, I entreat you will most carefully investigate the principles by which ascendency over others is secured and influence exerted, and labor to attain this qualification, on which success preëminently depends, or leave to others this important field of labor.

9. *Tact* for teaching is another essential qualification. This depends very much on ability to discern what ought to be done, and how that may be most readily accomplished. It involves considerable acquaintance with the characteristics of mind, with the diversities of schools, and great familiarity with the subjects claiming attention in school. "The best education is not that which accumulates the greatest amount of information and skill in any department of science or art, but that which gives to all the mental and moral powers the fullest and most symmetrical development." Tact for teaching will enable one to adapt everything most fully to this end. Things to be attained, the means that are to be employed, and the classification of these means, must be before the mind. The same means are not to be resorted to at all times, any more than the same medicine in all diseases. Tact in teaching, is an ability to apprehend the best means in view of the circumstances, and the ready application of these means for the attainment of the desired result. This qualification is *essential.* There is a "*best way*" to accomplish almost any object. That "best way" should be earnestly sought after by the instructor.

Very nearly allied to tact in teaching, is tact in managing, a school; that is, ability to act under the various circumstances in which you may be placed, so as most easily to remove difficulties, and to turn everything to the best account, for the good of the school. As intimated in a former Lecture, there will be found more or less difficulties or obstacles in almost every district. These are so various, that no previous description will apply to them all, and no previously formed plans will meet the exigency in every case. The teacher must be able to examine the character and bearing of each one as it occurs, and also the resources within reach, either for removing or surmounting it. These very evils, by the ingenious teacher, may be even sometimes so directed, as to be turned to good account, in gaining an important end. I can in no way better illustrate this, than by a quotation from Mr. Abbott. He says: "I know of nothing which illustrates more perfectly the way by which a knowledge of human nature is to be turned to account in managing human minds, than a plan which was adopted for clearing the galleries of the British House of Commons, as it was described to me by a gentleman who had visited London. It is well known that the gallery is appropriated to spectators, and that it sometimes becomes necessary to order them to retire, when a vote is to be taken or private business is to be transacted. When the officer in attendance was ordered to clear the gallery, it was sometimes found to be a very troublesome and slow operation; for those who went out first remained obstinately as close to the doors as possible, so as to secure the opportunity to come in again first when the doors should be reopened. The consequence was, there was so great an accumulation around the doors outside, that it was almost impossible for the crowd to get out. The whole difficulty arose from the eager desire of every one to get as near as possible to the door, *through which they were to come back again.* I have been told, that, notwithstanding the utmost efforts of the officers, fifteen minutes were sometimes consumed in effecting the object, when the order was given that the spectators should retire. The whole difficulty was obviated by a very simple plan. One door only was opened when the crowd was to retire, and they were then admitted through the other. The consequence was, that, as soon as the order was given to clear the galleries, every one fled as fast as possible through the open door around to the one which was closed, so as to be ready to enter first when that in its turn should be opened; this was usually in a few minutes, as the purpose for which the spectators were ordered to retire was usually simply to allow time for taking a vote. Here it will be seen that, by the operation of a very simple plan, the very eagerness of the crowd to get back as soon as possible, which had been the sole cause of the difficulty, was turned to account most effectually to remove it. Before, they were so eager to return, that they crowded around the door so as to prevent others going out. But, by this simple plan of ejecting them by one door and admitting them by another, that very circumstance made them clear the passage at once, and hurried every one away into the lobby, the moment the command was given.

"The planner of this scheme must have taken great pleasure in seeing its successful operation; though the officer who should go steadily on, endeavoring to remove the reluctant throng by dint of mere driving, might well have found his task most unpleasant. But the exercise of ingenuity in studying the nature of the difficulty with which a man has to contend, and bringing in some antagonist principle of human nature to remove it, or, if not an antagonist principle, a similar principle, operating by a peculiar arrangement of circumstances in an antagonist manner, is always pleasant. From this source a large share of the enjoyment which men find in the active pursuits of life has its origin."

Every mind is so constituted as to take a positive pleasure in the exercise of ingenuity in adapting means to an end, and in watching their operations; in accomplishing, by the intervention of instruments, what we could not accomplish without; in devising — when we see an object to be effected which is too great for our *direct* and *immediate* power — and setting at work some instrumentality, which may be sufficient to accomplish it.

It is said that when the steam engine was first put into operation, such was the imperfection of the machinery, that a boy was necessarily stationed at it, to open and shut alternately the cock, by which the steam was now admitted, and now shut out, from the cylinder. One such boy, after patiently doing his work for many days, contrived to connect this stopcock with some of the moving parts of the engine, by a wire, in such a manner, that the engine itself did the work which had been intrusted to him; and after seeing that the whole business would go regularly forward, he left the wire in charge, and went away to play. Such is the story. Now, if it is true, how much pleasure that boy must have experienced in devising and witnessing the successful operation of his scheme.

Looking at an object to be accomplished, or an evil to be remedied, then studying its nature and extent, and devising and executing some means for effecting the purpose desired, is, in all cases, a source of pleasure. This is peculiarly the case with experiments upon mind, or experiments for producing effects through the medium of voluntary acts of the human mind, so that the contriver must take into consideration the laws of mind in forming his plans. To illustrate this by rather a childish case: I once knew a boy who was employed by his father to remove all the loose small stones, which, from the peculiar nature of the ground, had accumulated in the road before the house. He was to take them up, and throw them over into the pasture across the way. He soon got tired of picking them up by one by one, and sat down upon the bank, to try and devise some better means of accomplishing his work. He at length conceived and adopted the following plan. He set up in the pasture a narrow board, for a target, or, as boys would call it, a *mark;* and then, collecting all the boys of the neighborhood, he proposed to them an amusement which boys are always ready for,—firing at a mark. I need not say, that the stores of ammunition in the street were soon exhausted; the boys *working for their leader*, when they supposed they were only finding *amusement for themselves.*

The teacher has the whole field which this subject opens, fully before him. He has human nature to deal with most directly. His whole work is experimenting upon mind; and the mind which is before him, to be the subject of his operation, is exactly in the state to be most easily and pleasantly operated upon. The reason, now, why some teachers find their work delightful, and some find it wearisomeness and tedium itself, is, that some do and some do not take this view of their work. One instructor is like the engine-boy, turning, without cessation or change, his everlasting stopcock, in the same ceaseless, mechanical, and monotonous routine. Another is like the little workman in his brighter moments, fixing his invention, and watching with delight its successful and easy accomplishment of his wishes. One is like the officer, driving by vociferation and threats, and demonstrations of violence, the spectators from the galleries. The other, like the shrewd contriver, who converts the very cause which was the whole ground of the difficulty to a most successful and efficient cause of its removal.

These principles show why teaching may in

some cases be a delightful employment, while in others its *tasteless dulness* is interrupted by nothing but its *perplexities* and *cares*. The school-room is, in reality, a little empire of mind. If the one who presides in it sees it in its true light, studies the nature and tendency of the minds which he has to control, adapts his plans and his measures to the laws of human nature, and endeavors to accomplish his purposes for them, not by mere labor and force, but by ingenuity and enterprise, he will take pleasure in administering his little government. He will watch, with care and interest, the operation of the moral and intellectual causes which he sets in operation, and find, as he will accomplish with increasing facility and power his various objects, that he will derive a greater and greater pleasure from his work. Now when a teacher thus looks upon his school as a field in which he is to exercise skill and ingenuity and enterprise; when he studies the laws of human nature, and the character of those minds upon which he is to act; when he explores deliberately the nature of the field which he has to cultivate, and of the objects which he wishes to accomplish; and applies means judiciously and skilfully adapted to the object; he must necessarily take a strong interest in his work. But when, on the other hand, he goes to his employment only to perform a certain regular round of daily work, undertaking nothing and anticipating nothing but this dull and unchangeable routine; and when he looks upon his pupils merely as passive objects, of his labors, whom he is to treat with simple indifference while they obey his commands, and to whom he is to apply reproaches and punishment when they disobey; such a teacher can never take pleasure in his school. Weariness and dulness must reign in both master and scholars, when things as he imagines are going right, and mutual anger and crimination when they go wrong.

In many of these illustrations may be seen the value of the talent which I have named. I might illustrate in many other ways, but shall content myself with one or two.

A teacher found his scholars very tardy in arriving at school in the morning. He reproved it, but the evil was not checked; he threatened, and even punished a few, but it grew worse and worse, so that hardly any one of his school regulations could be fully executed, and scarcely one of his classes was ready at the time assigned for an exercise. How shall the evil be remedied? He may punish them more severely. But then, he has business for the day; besides, the scholars were those who attended school most of the year, and did not realize that tardiness was a crime of much magnitude, or the occasion of much loss. Inflicting punishment will *not* secure the removal of the evil. Well, then, complain to the parents, and have them see that the children are in season; but the parents have other business, more than they can attend to, and tell the teacher he is hired to take care of the children: he must punish them, or contrive some other way to make them prompt. What shall he do? After losing a night's sleep in planning and thinking over the subject, he devises this plan: —

I will mark all the scholars who are in at nine o'clock, and those shall be dismissed fifteen minutes before four o'clock, P. M. Those who come in between nine and fifteen minutes after, shall stay till quarter past four o'clock. Those not in then, and that are in at half-past nine, shall be dismissed at half-past four, and those who enter later, not till five o'clock. What was the result? Why, after a few days, all were in at nine, or before that hour. Scarcely a scholar was tardy.

Now this teacher had a serious evil to overcome, but he contrived to make the children's love for play the means of correcting it. He studied the philosophy of mind, and by this means was enabled to accomplish his object.

Take another illustration. A teacher in the country often suffered for want of wood. The parents had agreed to furnish a quarter of a cord for each scholar. One wished to furnish it next week, and another the week after, etc. The supply was irregular; the scholars were cold; there was danger that the school must stop. How shall the evil be remedied? He resorted to the following plan. He went to a bachelor who owned a good team, and bargained with him for as much wood as he should need, and engaged his team on the next Saturday, to draw wood, provided he should need it. On Wednesday, he remarked to the school, that, as they had been troubled about wood, he supposed those who were to see to it were very much engaged in other business, and probably many might be unable to procure it in season. It is so important to you that we should have a supply on hand, I have concluded not to keep school next Saturday, and as I am fond of a day's exercise now and then, I have hired Mr. Willoby's team to draw wood. Perhaps some of the large scholars will be willing to go and chop. All who can, and would like to join me, may tell me to-morrow morning.

The teacher uttered no complaint, spoke in his usual good-natured manner; did not ask the scholars to repeat his remarks to parents or others, but just told his plan as he would speak of any common business matter. He intended to do as he had said, if there should be an occasion for it, and he meant to do it cheerfully. But he expected that, if the people of the district were like other people, this course would bring him a wood-pile. What was the result? The scholars mentioned the subject incidentally at home, and several made up their minds to join the "wood-bee." But those parents who were in fault began to think about it, and at last to inquire, "How will this look, and how will it sound, that the master is obliged to dismiss his school, to go out and get up wood?" It did not seem just right, and before night on Friday, there was a generous woodpile at the door of the school-house, and all the teacher had to say to the school was, merely, that if he had known that Thursday and Friday were the days to draw the wood, he should not have spoken for a team to get up some. The next winter the wood was drawn and cut up before the school began.

Now this teacher knew just how to act under existing circumstances, and to act in a judicious manner in regard to them. But had he complained, spoken unkindly about the parents, etc., it is not probable that the woodpile would have been found there.

The still small voice often accomplishes what the earthquake, fire, wind, and tempest fail to do. Young ladies and gentlemen, study this subject. There is always some way to turn in every exigency. Let me add one word of advice on all such occasions. Be CALM, be GOOD-NATURED, and then go to work in earnest. A mountain *may* be tunnelled that cannot be removed.

LECTURE V.

YOUNG LADIES AND GENTLEMEN: —

IN previous Lectures, I have spoken of qualifications of teachers, with regard to several things which have no very direct reference to literary attainments. The suggestions of several of those elements of character, necessarily imply the duties devolving on instructors. In this and following Lectures, I design to speak of those qualifications which have more particular reference to literature and science, in connection with the best modes of communicating instruction.

In conducting the studies of those qualifying themselves to become instructors, I have uniformly recommended that every branch should be studied with reference, not only to obtaining a thorough knowledge of that particular subject, but its relation to other branches, and also the best mode of teaching it. This course I most earnestly recommend to you. Many who teach fail of success, because, while they attempted to acquire a knowledge of a particular branch, so as to understand it themselves, they neglected to investigate its relations to other branches, and to inquire, how most successfully to communicate a knowledge of it to others. Those who would teach well, ought not only to be familiar with the subject, but know how to impart that knowledge to others in the shortest time and the most thorough manner.

The number of branches specified by the law establishing district or common schools, is generally limited to spelling, reading, writing, arithmetic, geography, and English grammar. In some instances, history of the United States is very properly included. But allow me to state here, that a thorough knowledge of these particular branches requires familiarity with several others. Ability to give instruction in these, in the *best manner*, is only acquired by those who have made other attainments. As teachers of primary schools, from the nature of their employment, must ordinarily lay the foundation on which those who come after them are to build, they should be familiar with the first principles of science. They should know both *what* to teach, and how to teach, each particular branch in the best manner. But with regard to this general qualification, there is, I am obliged to say, general deficiency. This is more apparent with regard to some branches than others; most common, with regard to spelling and reading. Why it is so, I can hardly assign a reason, but I am obliged to say, that, among thousands of scholars who have been under my instruction, I have found but a limited number, who have been willing to take the pains necessary to become *good* spellers and *good* readers. I have no doubt this has been the experience of other teachers. I have found in my visits to primary schools generally, greater deficiency in the method of teaching reading than any other branch.

The author* of the English "School Teacher's Manual" remarks, and certainly not without sufficient reason: "It has been observed that very few persons read well! To read simply and naturally, with animation and expression, is indeed a high and rare attainment. What is generally called *good reading* is, in fact, the very worst kind of reading; I mean, that which calls the attention of the auditor from the subject of discourse, to the supposed taste and skill of the person who is

* Rev. Henry Dunn.

pronouncing it *Ars est celare artena;* the perfection of art, is to conceal art. The best window is that which least intercepts the prospect; and he is the best reader, who brings before us the mind of the author, unincumbered by the tints and tracery of his own style and manner. Still, it must be remembered that, with most persons, reading is *an art.* The best readers are those who have most diligently studied their art; studied it so well, that you do not perceive they have ever studied it at all. You so thoroughly understand, and so sensibly feel, the force of *what* they say, that you never think for a moment *how* they are saying it, and you never know the exact extent of your obligation to the care and labor of the elocutionist. In many schools, little can be done beyond teaching the pupil to read in a plain and intelligent manner; to pronounce with general correctness, and to avoid offensive tones."

But if this is all that can be secured in any English schools, it is not all that ought to be done in *our* schools. The time that most scholars are allowed to attend school is amply sufficient, if they are properly instructed, to secure much more than this. But less than this is actually accomplished, in the majority of our best schools and best districts. So far as it depends on you, let this reproach cease. Qualify yourselves to read well, and then to teach others how to do so. Ability to read well is a rare attainment, and because it is so, it claims the more attention on the part of instructors.

Few intend to offer their services as school-teachers till they have made, at least in their own view, respectable attainments in arithmetic, geography, and in English grammar. A knowledge of these branches all regard as essential. Most are able to sustain a reputable examination in arithmetic and grammar. In geography, there is greater deficiency, owing more to defect in the text-books used, and to the mode of teaching adopted, than to negligence on the part of candidates. The great error is, an attempt is made to acquire *so much*, that nothing is thoroughly learned. Most who study geography, attempt to acquire a knowledge of so many things, that they fail of gaining a *thorough* knowledge of any. Much time is nearly wasted in this way; and the evil is continued from year to year, because the origin of it seems not to be generally apprehended.

On the subject of writing, I am sorry to be constrained to say, few only are willing to qualify themselves to teach; few only are willing to take the necessary pains to become good or elegant chirographers. On this subject, however, what I wish to say will be more appropriate in suggestions on the mode of teaching.

With a knowledge of the subjects before mentioned, teachers may be enabled to answer the *letter* of the law. But it seems plain to me, that some other branches are requisite, in order that they may be properly qualified to engage in directing the studies and disciplining the minds of the young.

Among these, I shall mention some acquaintance with natural history, the constitution of the United States, and of the State in which they live; rhetoric, natural philosophy, chemistry, and moral philosophy.

Some knowledge of natural history is important, to enable teachers to make other exercises more interesting. Geography has relation to botany, mineralogy, conchology, and zoology. Much interesting and valuable instruction on these subjects may be imparted by teachers, not only without hindering progress in other branches, but making it more rapid.

No subjects present greater attractions to the young mind, or are better calculated to cultivate habits of thought and investigation. Such an acquaintance with these sciences, as will enable you to present their most interesting features, will prepare you to converse with your pupils on a variety of interesting and important topics. By this they may be led to examine, compare, and think for themselves, and take lessons from almost every object around them. A *picture* has charms for children found in few other things. They usually listen to simple and intelligible descriptions of the objects of which they have any knowledge with great satisfaction. Seldom will a child be found, who is not willing to leave his *play*, to hear you tell a story about a mineral, an animal, or even an insect. I have often seen children three or four years old, listen to a story on some subject in natural history, with an eagerness of attention not surpassed by those of any age. You have observed in children, the pleasure with which they hear the stories of the nursery. If this curiosity, this passion for novelty, thus early developed, receive a right direction from teachers, it may be made a powerful instrument for good. But if there is a deficiency of the requisite knowledge; if teachers have not materials in their minds, by the aid of which they may make such communications instructive as well as interesting, they must lose many opportunities of usefulness.

Teachers should be familiar with the constitution of the United States, because it is necessary frequently to refer the young to the Bill of Rights, by which their privileges are secured. The earlier children are made acquainted with this, the more likely will they be to respect the law, and yield a cheerful obedience to it. It is important that every child should be told something of the constitution of his own State. The instructor should be acquainted with it, in order to call the attention of youth to those subjects in which they have a common interest. If Hannibal was old enough at nine years of age, "to take an oath that he would never be at peace with the Romans," our children, at school, are old enough to have their attention turned to the principles of the government which they are to support.

Rhetoric is a subject with which the instructor ought to be acquainted, because he ought to assist his scholars in arranging their thoughts in sentences, and committing them to paper. The older scholars, in all our schools, should be instructed in *letter-writing* and *composition*. To be able to write a letter, or to express one's thoughts on any subject that may claim attention, is highly important. It is what every one will, more or less frequently, have occasion to do. If some attention be not given to this, at school, there will be mortification and regret in after life. Our children ought to be taught *that* at school, which they will most need in the common business and duties of manhood. A knowledge of rhetoric is necessary to enable teachers to *correct* the compositions of their scholars, and to give them such rules for the arrangement of sentences, as shall be a guide to them in their early efforts.

Some acquaintance with natural philosophy, and the first principles of chemistry, enables the instructor to explain to pupils many facts which will rouse their curiosity, and excite a thirst for more knowledge on these interesting subjects. Many facts are frequently observed by young children, the reason of which they are not able to understand, but which they have capacity to comprehend, if a familiar illustration were given. Those appearances, frequently, which excite no attention, on account of their commonness, would awaken very high interest, if explained in a familiar manner. Such are the turning of a wheel, the power of a wedge, or screw, the freezing of water, the formation of clouds, rain, and snow, the transmission of sound, etc., etc. What the young most need, is, to learn *how to learn;* to think, and to investigate for themselves. Whatever serves to form a habit of reflection is of incalculable importance. By some simple illustration, the attention of the child may often become interested, and a train of thoughts excited, not less important to himself, than that sublime theory suggested to Newton by the fall of an apple. Instructors have many opportunities to direct the attention of their scholars to the first principles of natural science, without diverting it from other subjects of study. He should certainly possess that knowledge of these branches which will enable him thus to impart instruction and delight to those under his care.

I mentioned moral philosophy as one of the branches with which instructors should be familiar. I am well aware that this study is much neglected. But having been neglected heretofore, furnishes no reason why it should be neglected still. If a man were guided by instinct alone, to the attainment of his best good, the theory of morals would be less important. Every one knows he may fail of this, either by inaction or by ill-directed effort. "He finds himself led astray by his passions; and he looks in vain, for a safe guide, to the example of others. It is, then, the dictate of wisdom, to inquire by what means these wayward propensities may be subdued, and the foot be guided in the paths of peace. Happy are they who are led to make this inquiry in their early years. Happier are they, whom the hand of instruction, before they are able to make the inquiry for themselves, has been guiding in the path of knowledge and virtue." * This is the appropriate work of the parent and the primary school teacher. But, alas, how many parents wholly neglect it! Hence a greater responsibility devolves on the teacher. "Moral philosophy," says Dr. Paley, "is that science which teaches men their duty, and the reasons of it." This, then, is the knowledge "which the young most need, and which the friendly instructor should sedulously impart. It is this, "which tends to recall us from low pursuits; to fix our affections on better objects; to form us to such a character, and direct us to such a course of conduct, as will secure the divine approbation, and be most promotive of our own happiness and that of the community of which we are members. It teaches a knowledge of ourselves, of human nature in general, of our Creator, and of the relations we sustain to him, and to our fellow-creatures." Can any one, then, be properly qualified to train the infant mind, who has not some acquaintance with this science?

I am aware that, in the foregoing remarks on the qualifications of teachers, some may think the standard too elevated. But it will be said by none, surely, who have carefully investigated the necessities of the rising generation, or the influence for good or evil primary teachers exert. I have not placed the standard too high, when it is borne

---

* Parkhurst.

in mind that " teachers are in danger of mistaking the *end* and *object* of education, supposing it to consist in a mere attainment of knowledge, or the treasuring up of the opinions, sayings, or doings of others, irrespective of their use or application.

" Education consists in the formation of the character; and a *good* education involves the right development, cultivation, and direction, of all man's powers; physical, intellectual, and moral. It implies not only instruction in all the branches of knowledge which are necessary to useful and efficient action, in the sphere of the individual; but it must also include the *physical training* which is to render the body capable of executing the purposes of the soul; and the *skill* which is requisite, in order to apply our knowledge and strength to the very best advantage; and above all, the *moral training*, by which the character and direction of our efforts are to be decided." *

LECTURE VI.

YOUNG LADIES AND GENTLEMEN: —

SEVERAL other topics demand consideration. To these allow me to ask special attention.

1. Employ all available means to become tho-

---

* Galloup.

roughly acquainted with the nature of your duties and responsibilities.

This is important, first, to your personal enjoyment. We cannot be happy, when we do not know what to do, or how to act. To engage in a business of which you have no adequate idea, must, therefore, subject you to much unhappiness. The situation of an instructor is very responsible. It is exceedingly important that you should be acquainted with the nature and amount of this responsibility, and of the leading duties which will devolve on you, when placed at the head of a school. Without some knowledge of the duties you have to perform, the perplexities and difficulties that may arise, and the constant care that must then press upon you, you cannot but experience much inquietude and uneasiness. The very different temperaments of those you have to teach and govern, and the wide difference of treatment they have received from parents at home, may give you much trouble, if you awake to the reality of your situation only when a mountain of care presses upon you.

Form not expectations that cannot be realized, for disappointment will not only make you unhappy at the time, but will unfit you for the duties pressing at the moment. The nature of your business should, as far as possible, be learned beforehand. This is dictated by reason, and experience certainly confirms it. No one engages in any department of manual labor, till he has gained some knowledge of its details. No one commences a journey, till has learned the direction he is to go, and the probable character of the road, and of the people he is to find upon the way. No one proposes emigration to a distant part of the country, till he has made diligent inquiry as to the conveniences and privileges, as well as the privations and hardships, which will attend a removal. "Who goeth a warfare, till he has counted the cost? or begins to build a temple, till he has considered whether he be able to finish it?" The reason is obvious. When we expect hardship, we are prepared to endure it with *patience;* when we look for trial, we can meet it with comparative composure. If I foresee that the journey I am to take will be attended with great fatigue, I can bear it without complaint. If I expect the road I am to travel is one of exceeding roughness, I can endure its asperities without a murmur.

But if on the other hand I expect a distance of ten miles and it proves fifteen, if I expect a good road and it proves a bad one, it will appear both longer and worse than it really is; and what I might have borne with composure if anticipated, I cannot endure without disquietude and disappointment. If I expect to arrive at home in an hour, and it take two, the *last hour* will seem longer than *two*, ordinarily; for I am disappointed, and disappointment makes me unhappy. It gives everything around me an unpleasant aspect.

In the same way, disappointment in regard to the nature of your business as teachers, will have an important effect on your enjoyment. For, if you form only ideal notions; if you expect, in spite of evidence to the contrary, that everything will be "perfectly pleasant;" if you suppose the labor to be performed easy, and nothing to render it difficult and disagreeable, you will be entirely unprepared to bear the trials invariably attendant upon it. When these trials come, you will experience disappointment, which will make you unhappy at the time, and of course unfit you for the duties of the hour. In a discontented state, you are not prepared to proceed with that which, at another time, might be perfectly easy. Nor are you prepared, in this state, to enjoy what is usually pleasant and agreeable. It is generally true, that we bear unexpected difficulties with *far less* composure than when we had anticipated them, and of course made up our minds to bear them.

I do not assert that you can learn everything fully, in regard to the nature of your employment, without *experience.* It is not possible, in this or other callings. The physician, attorney, and minister, do not expect it. But they still use all the means within their reach, to become acquainted with the nature of their several professions, as far as may be, before entering upon them. This is as necessary for the teacher as for them.

Do you inquire how this can be done? I would say, first, read whatever has been written to which you can gain access. Within a few years, the periodical press has furnished much that is valuable. All the publications of the American Institute of Instruction are highly valuable, as before intimated.

Again, you may learn something of your business, by observing the peculiarities of children. They are men in miniature. Like men, they have their prepossessions and aversions. Some that come under your care have been governed at home; others have not. Recur again to the remarks in a previous Lecture on these diversities, and especially on *precocity* and *dulness*. You may derive assistance also, in learning the nature of your business, by reflecting on the great variety of character among parents. Some will wish you to govern the school, others will wish to *govern you.* One parent wishes you to be very strict, another to be very lenient. Some will wish you to use the rod with your scholars, others dread nothing so much as that their favorite children should feel the "rod of correction." Some will wish you to pursue a certain mode, others will be strong advocates for a system entirely different. Some will wish you to close early, others will fear that you will not keep your "hours." One will admonish you to show no partiality, and another will solicit very particular attention to *his* children. Mr. A is willing to trust the school entirely to your management, while Mr. B is very jealous, lest you assume more than your "delegated" authority. Some will be very anxious to have the school successful, others will be entirely indifferent. Some will cheerfully furnish all the necessary books, while others will think it enough to send their children to school without any, or with such as are entirely unfit for use. Some will be ready to listen to every complaint of their children, and others will teach them to "tell no tales out of school." The wealthy may perhaps think *their* children entitled to more attention than those of the poor, and the latter may be ready to imagine such a distinction *is* made, even if none really exist. In this enumeration, I have not mentioned a single thing which I have not had personal opportunity to observe; and in regard to many of them, have noticed the same thing in many different places. This diversity among children and among parents, renders it very necessary for you to reflect much, on the manner of securing that influence with both which will enable you to benefit all in the greatest degree. You must be prepared to govern your scholars at school, and *may* often find it necessary to exert nearly as much influence with *parents* as with them.

You may also learn something of the nature of your business, by frequent conversation with older teachers. They will be able to impart to you the results of their own experience. Be not disheartened, if they tell you of "strong prejudice" against every innovation which you may find it necessary to make; that with some, reason is but a name, and that every attempt to influence them by it will be as unsuccessful as that of Canute to rule the sea. "There is," they will tell you, "an almost universal disposition to believe, that books for study, methods of learning and teaching, common long ago, must be as good, at least, as any now in use. The spirit of inquiry, awakened within a few years past, is entirely unknown to the great mass of the people, who read but little, and have had no opportunity to investigate the character of proposed improvements, or to witness the results of successful experiments."

2. Another duty devolving on you is, to ascertain the best mode of communicating instruction. An English writer remarks: "You will readily perceive that this is an attainment perfectly distinct from any particular plan or system; and also a very different thing from what is usually termed *tact in teaching*. It is, in fact, the art of *so* communicating knowledge, that the pupil shall, as far as possible, comprehend, in all its relations, the truth sought to be imparted; and that, associating what is thus received with other and previous acquisitions, he may be led at one and the same time to cultivate his original faculties, and to store his mind richly and permanently with valuable facts. This is what I mean by the 'art of teaching,' a talent which few naturally possess, but which may doubtless be acquired by the careful and diligent study of the human mind, in connection with a moderate share of 'practice.'

"The use of this latter word suggests an analogy, which certainly to some extent subsists between the profession of teaching and that of medicine. He who would be an accomplished physician, must study *principles*, as well as 'see cases;' and, in like manner, he who would be a useful teacher, must look beyond the systems to the principles on which they rest. The man who thinks himself qualified to teach, merely because he has observed others teaching on a particular plan, is just as much an empiric as the medical pretender, whose course of study has been limited to occasional walks through the wards of an hospital. It was in connection with this view of the subject (its relation to the philosophy of the human mind), that Dr. Thomas Brown of Edinburgh, spoke of the art of teaching as 'the *noblest*, and, in proportion to its value, the *least studied*, of all the arts.' When examined in this light, it cannot fail, I think, to be recognized as an attainment worthy of patient study and earnest attention.

"Actuated by a sincere desire to communicate instruction in the best possible way, if, when entering your school-room, perplexed and harassed by the waywardness and indifference of your pupils; in this state of mind, you put the question, 'What can I do to excite attention, to stimulate dulness, to awaken effort?' I reply, as preliminary, indeed, to everything else, bring distinctly before your own mind the well-known fact, that *children delight as much in exercising their minds as their limbs;* provided only that which is presented to them be suited to their capacities, and adapted to their strength.

"It is a great mistake to suppose, as many do, that, in order to make learning pleasant to the young, difficulties must as much as possible be removed out of the way. On the contrary, it is in teaching them to *overcome* difficulties that we shall be most likely to create the interest we are so desirous of calling forth. As a general rule, it should be the care of a teacher to supply his pupils, from day to day, with a succession of topics, somewhat *beyond their knowledge without being above their comprehension.*"

Many have appeared to imbibe the sentiment, that the whole business of instruction consists in keeping order in the school-room, and going through a daily round of exercises in reading, spelling, and writing, perhaps furnishing copies, making pens, and performing certain operations in arithmetic, which the students may not be able to perform themselves. But all this has little better claim to the name of teaching, than the chatter of a magpie to language. Such a course may be as mechanical as the operation of a machine. Let it be well fixed in your mind, that *to teach, is to communicate ideas.* It is indispensable that you should be *understood.* The words of an experienced teacher* are in point: "Use language that your scholars can understand. Let your illustrations be drawn from topics within their knowledge. It is entirely out of place, in a common elementary school, to use the language of a professor in the university, or to *affect* the use of terms understood only by the more advanced student. If you teach *children*, use the language of children. Let it be pure and grammatical; but you convey no instruction, if it be above their comprehension. When you compare

* Mr. Rand.

a thing unknown with another thing equally unknown, how can the child be the wiser for it? In talking with your scholars, use their own phraseology, and condescend to their capacities." Teachers should put themselves in the place of the child, and then inquire what course it would be necessary for them to take, to gain a knowledge of any subject with which they are not familiar. No means within your reach, for learning the nature of your business, should be left unemployed. If all which are desirable are not accessible, those which are should be used with the greater fidelity.

3. Consider the responsibility of the station you are to occupy. If, in deciding to devote yourself to the employment of teaching, you have been excited by the hope that it will be less arduous than other employments in which you might have engaged, you have doubtless mistaken the nature of its duties and cares, and the very first day of your trial will dissipate the delusion. The sight of a company of blooming children and youth, "awed by your presence, waiting for your directions, and turning their inquiring eyes on you, to guide them in acquiring knowledge and forming habits," will tell you, in language more forcible than any I can use, that on you devolves an arduous task; to you, parents are confiding an important trust; to you, your country is committing a solemn charge.

The responsibility of your situation may be realized in some measure, by considering that children have minds naturally dark, which are to be enlightened,—are ignorant of that which they most need to know, and must be instructed. They are tender twigs, ready to receive any direction that may be given them. They are miniature men, destined soon to occupy the places of those who are now active on the stage of life. Yes, in the little community with which you are surrounded, there *may* be a Franklin or a Washington; or, on the other hand, a Robespierre or a Bonaparte, or Joseph Smith, according to the cast of character which they receive from you. In a country like ours, where character is the passport to the most important stations in society, and where offices are open to every one who shows himself worthy of the confidence of the people, the responsibility of the teacher is even higher than in those countries where estates and offices are hereditary. He who is selected to educate a prince, even in the first rudiments of science, considers his station as highly responsible. But in a country like our own, instructors should consider responsibility equally great or greater. Yes, you at the same *moment* may be educating a president, a governor, a general, a judge, a minister, physician, lawyer, senator, and counsellor. Who can tell what results may be produced by the influence you may exert on either of these? But suppose none of your scholars should ever fill these important stations, yet the station of *every one* who becomes a voter, and sustains simply the character of a citizen, is important. Such you most certainly will have. Over these your power must be great.

You may learn your responsibility by considering the *influence which you may exert* over your youthful charge. I have said in a former Lecture, children are inclined to regard the teacher they love as being almost perfect. If you succeed in gaining their love, your influence will be greater in some respects than that of parents themselves. It will be in your power to direct them in almost any path you choose. You may lead them to form habits of application and industry, or permit them to form those of idleness and indifference. You may win them either to a love for learning and respect for virtue, or, by your negligence and unfaithfulness, you may suffer them to become regardless of both. You have power to lead them to a cultivation of the social affections; kindness, benevolence, and humanity; or, by your neglect, they may become the reverse of everything that is lovely, amiable, and generous. It will be in your power greatly to assist them in learning to make just distinctions in the examination of the principles of moral conduct; and to govern their own actions accordingly; or you may, by your unfaithfulness, suffer them to contract the habit of pursuing, regardless of consequences, everything they desire, as impelled by passion; and opposing with temper everything that counteracts their wishes. You may teach them the duty of yielding submission to proper authority and law, or, by suffering them to disregard authority and trample on laws with impunity, teach them to oppose all restraint, and consider all law as unnecessary and oppressive. You may do something towards leading them to cultivate that public spirit, so essential to the well-being of citizens of a free country, or you may train them in those habits of selfishness, which will unfit them to be members of a republic, or civil community.

If the consequences of your influence over them were to cease in *this* world, your responsibility would be less, far less, than it actually is. But no. Revelation assures us, that our future condition will be decided by the character formed in time,—that man will be rewarded in the world to come, "according to the deeds done in this." The formation of character is not then a matter important in relation to *this life only*. The children with whom you are to be associated are all the children of one great Creator,—a part of his extensive kingdom. They are the subjects of his government, and are under the highest obligation to obey his wise and holy laws. He has given them such laws, and made such requirements of them, as are necessary for their happiness. He has enjoined upon them to "Remember their Creator in the days of their youth," and "to love their neighbor as themselves;" to honor and obey their parents. He has prohibited profaneness and falsehood. He has enjoined the duty of gratitude to the Saviour, and of repentance for sin. Each individual committed to your care is liable every day to be called away from this world, to render up an account of the "deeds done in the body." The influence you will exert over them, by your example and instructions, may deeply affect them in regard to these solemn considerations. And as their happiness, present and eternal, depends on the temper they exhibit in regard to the character and laws of Jehovah, if you are so happy as to lead them to love him, how great the benefit you may confer upon them. But if, by your example and instruction, you lead them away from the paths of wisdom, how great the injury! They will be more likely to listen to counsel and advice from a beloved teacher, than from almost any other person. They will generally be more disposed to regard what you say to them on the subject of their moral obligation, than what is said to them by their parents or their minister. This talent which you are permitted to occupy, is one for the improvement of which you are accountable. And how much does it increase the interest of your calling! Hence, I should be guilty of unfaithfulness, did I neglect to direct your attention to your own moral obligation. You, as well as the youth committed to your charge, have an account to render to him who gave you your existence. If you are put in possession of an influence, which, if properly exerted, may greatly augment individual happiness, as well as that of the nation; or, on the other hand, if not properly exerted, may in the same ratio increase the amount of human misery; fail not to ponder well the subject which is to throw upon you so important responsibility. And fail not to ask wisdom of him "who gives liberally and upbraids not."

He only is able to guide you right, and keep you from error, and give that wisdom without which all will err and come short.

4. Let me invite your earnest attention to another subject; the means by which you may gain a controlling influence over all the young placed under your charge.

You cannot have failed to observe, that persons in similar situations exert very different degrees of influence. This is observable among men in every station. Those of equal natural talent, when placed in stations of authority, exhibit this strongly. One has great influence, and his wish or will is undisputed law; another has but little, if any. This you have no doubt often seen verified among parents, and in families. It is equally exhibited in schools. To all that is said by one teacher, great deference is paid; another can hardly secure the attention of scholars to anything he may say. For this wide difference there is some reason. What is it?

In a Lecture before the American Institute, Mr. Howard observes: "There is an air of authority about some men, which at once commands respect and compels obedience. This was remarkably true of the beloved and venerated Washington. Even Aaron Burr, proverbially bold and impudent as he was, could never take the slightest liberty with him."

In other cases there may be those who have similar power, with no apparent effort on their part. But however this may be, in some cases it is doubtless true, that this power may be in a measure acquired. If so, it becomes a matter of great importance to instructors to cultivate it. In ascertaining what are the elements of this power, you may usefully recur to the instructors under whom you were placed. You will probably recollect that to some of them you listened with great deference; that you were anxious to please them, and desirous of gaining their good opinion, while to the esteem of others you were indifferent, and careless whether you gained their good-will or not. To meet with some of them *now*, affords you great pleasure; while to meet with others, is a source of no satisfaction. And what is the reason? You will answer, that these exhibited very different traits of character; that they showed very different degrees of interest in their business; that they possessed very different qualifications for their duties, and evinced different degrees of solicitude for your welfare. Let me ask farther, what were those traits that pleased you, and pleased the school generally? Was the teacher pleasant and obliging, or morose and ill-humored? and with which was the school better pleased? Was the instructor affable and condescending, and proverbially punctual to time, to promises and to threats, or regardless of all? and on which of these accounts were you willing to be directed? Did the teacher appear affectionate and kind in intercourse, or seem to delight in giving you pain and fear? and with which of these traits of character were you better pleased? Did he convince you that he was your real friend, and desired your good, even at the expense of his own ease, or did he act as if he were the friend of no one but himself? Was he ever ready to assist you to the extent of his ability, or did he send you away without answering your reasonable questions or solving your doubts? Did he prove to you by his whole conduct, that he desired to benefit the school in the highest degree of which he was capable, or did he appear to regard little else than to obtain the stipulated reward? and on which account do you now remember him with affection and interest?

You are at no loss to decide such questions. Let them, then, serve as a directory to you, in making the inquiry, how *you* can secure that degree of confidence on the part of your scholars, which will enable you to benefit them in the highest degree. To secure this end, endeavor to convince the scholars *that you are their true friend;* that you aim at their improvement, and desire their best good. It will not take long to convince them of this, if you do so in reality; and if you pursue the course with them which would, when pursued by your own instructor, have excited this belief in you. Remember, however, that merely a declaration that you are their friend, will be very far from proving you to be such, or convincing them of it. You would not have been convinced by the mere declaration of your instructor to this effect. You must *prove* it to your pupils, by showing a greater regard for their welfare than for your own ease.

Secondly. In order to secure a proper degree of their confidence, *you must avoid being hasty.* Be not hasty to reprove, be not hasty to praise; be not hasty to promise, be not hasty to threaten; be not hasty to punish, and be not hasty to forget a real fault. There is somewhere an old proverb, "Haste makes waste, and waste brings want." Haste in schools, in any of the particulars specified, will bring want of confidence. Whatever is done in haste is seldom done well. In school, it must of necessity subject you frequently to the mortification of countermanding an order; of failing to fulfil your promise, or of exciting the belief in the minds of your scholars that you are forgetful. It is generally true that, in every situation, the deliberate man accomplishes the most; but in none is deliberation more important than in him who is to exercise authority over a large community. Loss of time is not, however, the greatest inconvenience of being hasty in school; there must be loss of confidence on the part of the scholars. You are well aware that you place but little confidence in any man who bears the character of being hasty, be his calling or station what it may. Be deliberate in all you do or say.

Thirdly. If you wish to secure the confidence of your school, never allow yourself *to speak angrily* or unusually *loud*, and be sure never "to *fret* or *scold*." All such things are disagreeable. And surely you cannot expect to secure the confidence of a school by indulging yourself in those habits which must make you disagreeable to every one. Mr. Howard remarks: "There are some general directions which suit every latitude, and are applicable to every teacher. And were I required to give to a teacher, in a few words, what I deem one of the most important of these general practical directions in establishing and maintaining good order in school, it should be, *Do not make much noise yourself;* and were I asked for a second and third, I would simply repeat it, DO NOT MAKE MUCH NOISE YOURSELF. A bustling, noisy teacher will always make a bustling, noisy school; and, in general, you will find the noise in a school in direct proportion to that which the teacher makes himself. I repeat it: *the noise in a school is generally in direct proportion to that which the teacher makes himself.*

"I have more than intimated that all the orders of the school should be given in a low, but distinct tone of voice. I will also add, that it is equally important that they should be expressed in few words, and not too often repeated. *Much talking always weakens authority.* I have known teachers repeat a command two or three times, without even allowing the scholar *time* to comply, however disposed to obedience he might be. And, mark it where you will, every repetition diminishes the force of a command. Even *reproof*, to have any effect, should be sparingly administered. The rules and directions of a school should be few and simple, and prompt and cheerful obedience should be quietly but firmly insisted upon."

Fourthly. You will secure the confidence of

the school, by being *punctual* in everything. Have a time for everything, and do everything at the right time. Punctuality in business of every kind, gains confidence. It prevents the loss of time, and secures opportunity for every duty. It is nowhere more important than in teaching. Without it, you can accomplish but little. If, after due deliberation, you make a promise, be sure to keep it. If you require a child to do this or that, see that it is done *exactly* as you require. If he has obeyed you but in part, it is little better than disobedience. By being punctual in fulfilling every promise, you will not be charged with falsifying your word. Your scholars will not ask a second time for any indulgence which you may once have denied them. They will know what you mean, when you say yes or no."

Finally. Be willing to devote your whole time, and strive to make the most judicious use of it. If you have made no reserve of any part of your time, the whole belongs to your employers. I know not that there is anything morally wrong in making an agreement to reserve a portion of time, to be devoted to your own purposes. But it does seem to me manifestly wrong, if no such agreement has been made with your employers, for you to use any considerable portion of it for your own private benefit, instead of that of the school. This rule ought to be observed, whether the school be large or small; whether your wages are high or low. If you have made an engagement for even less than a just compensation, this cannot alter your obligations to the children placed under your care. *They* are not to be injured, if their parents *have* misjudged in regard to what ought to be your hire. You had your choice whether to engage or not, and if you have consented to work for less compensation than you ought to receive, vour obligation is still the same as if you were to receive more. If you have engaged to keep the school without any reserve, you are under obligation to give your pupils all the time which you can render useful to them. This direction *may* seem to you unreasonable or impracticable. If so, I have only to ask you to examine it attentively; and if you shall then conclude that you cannot bring yourselves to adopt the spirit of it, I hope you will renounce the idea of teaching and choose some other business. I do not mean by this, to say that you ought not to take the time necessary for exercise and rest, and for answering the claims of friendship. This would be expected under any engagement whatever. It is expected in all other public employments, and it is equally proper in yours.

Some schools do make twice or three times as much progress as others. Most, might make double advancement to that really made. And if it be true that double the usual improvement might be made in district schools generally, the subject is one of no ordinary importance. Let me ask you to reflect on it a moment. Suppose the number of scholars in a school is forty. The time, board, wear of apparel, and use of books, cannot be estimated at less, for each, than one dollar and fifty cents per week. The wages and board of male teachers, at least, will amount to six dollars a week, and probably more. The school, then, costs sixty-six dollars a week, or two hundred and sixty-four dollars a month. If there are six such schools in a town, the expense of them is fifteen hundred and eighty-four dollars a month. Suppose each school is to continue two and a half months, the cost to the town is three thousand nine hundred and sixty dollars, for a single term. Now, if there is but half the improvement made that might be made, we cannot consider the actual pecuniary loss at less than half this sum. If, after looking at the subject in this light, any are unwilling to devote their whole time to the work, I will again make the request, that they turn their attention to some other employment, and not occasion so great a loss to the community. Leave the work to those who will enter upon it with greater spirit, and who are willing to spare no pains.

I have been led to the last suggestion, from having the conviction forced upon me, that many who have offered their services as teachers, have had no higher motive in so doing, than the attainment of a pecuniary reward. But while I am firm in the belief that the laborer is worthy of his hire, and while I also know that the ordinary compensation is lower than it ought to be, I cannot still conceive that any one ought to engage in this highly responsible business, merely for the sake of the compensation. In business less responsible it may be justifiable to make that the first object. But where an influence so important is to be exerted, — an influence that will probably affect the character and happiness of many, during the rest of their lives; it does seem to me that *patriotism*, to say nothing of higher inducements, requires that the first object of a teacher should be *to do good*, and that those only should engage in teaching, who are willing to devote the largest portion of their time that can be rendered beneficial to the school. How often is it said in our hearing, that "our school has done us no good;" that "it has been worse than none; that the money might as well have been thrown away." I will not charge *every* failure on instructors. It does not always belong to them; but I am persuaded that a great majority of the instances of failure in the success of schools, is to be in part attributed to teachers. Let every one engage earnestly in the work, and devote the whole time to the business, and such instances will be few and far between.

By observing these and similar principles, and acting in a manner corresponding to them, you will be able to gain such ascendency over your youthful charge as is necessary to enable you to benefit them. You will find it impossible to secure their confidence by any opposite course, for it is opposed to the principles of nature.

LECTURE VII.

Young Ladies and Gentlemen: —

Preceding considerations, it is hoped, will be adequate to fix in your minds just considerations of the object of your labors, and of the essential qualifications and general duties of instructors. I now invite attention to the general management of schools. The first topic of remark under this head, is *government*. I have before stated that ability to govern is a very essential qualification in a teacher, and have already given several of the reasons for it. You must govern your schools, or all other efforts on your part will be abortive. To the following suggestions I ask, therefore, particular attention.

The first thing on which success in governing a school depends, is ability to govern yourselves. If instructors cannot control themselves; if easily excited and thrown off their balance; if made fretful by trifling annoyance, or excited to anger by the misdemeanor of scholars, they cannot govern others. They cannot secure confidence and respect. Correction of real faults, if administered in anger, has no tendency to benefit the offender. It shows, even to a child, that he who administers it, is guilty of a fault as great as his own. Temptations to excitement will undoubtedly occur. A scholar may be impudent; from his ignorance of good manners, or in a sudden gust of passion, he may, perhaps, grossly insult you. Hardly anything is more apt to call forth anger, than an insult from an inferior. But still, the indulgence of anger is very unwise. If a pupil commit a fault, he ought certainly to be admonished or corrected; but if the teacher, by an unmanly indulgence of passion, descend to the level of a child, he *cannot* expect to benefit *him* materially by any correction whatever, administered in such a state of mind.

There is another particular in which it is very important you should govern yourselves. Be careful to make no contemptuous remarks concerning any of your pupils. Such remarks may excite a smile from the rest of the school, but it will not be the smile of approbation. The affections of that pupil you have lost, and every effort to benefit him by your instructions will probably do him very little good. You may and often will see things that might seem to give occasion for such remarks, but as your design is to *benefit* your scholars, avoid them. If the pupil make a careless blunder, he may be reproved calmly, but never should be made the butt of ridicule. It is of equal importance that you should govern yourselves in regard to such speeches about *families*.

You may see many things in family management to excite a smile, and many things which really deserve censure. But such censure does not come well from the instructor of their children. To be ridiculed by the teacher, will have little effect to correct improprieties. I cannot blame you for being diverted, sometimes, at what you may observe in family management. I know well that the eccentricity sometimes observable cannot fail to amuse or to vex you. But still, keep your reflections to yourselves.

Some of these points may appear of trifling importance to you, but much of your success in the business of teaching depends on things that to a superficial observer may appear small.

If you succeed in becoming able to govern yourselves, you will be prepared to govern those placed under your care. An important object will have been gained, when you have brought yourselves to feel that to govern the school is of primary importance, and that you *can* and *will* maintain proper discipline, and secure order. When you strongly cherish these feelings, your scholars will read them in your countenance. But the moment instructors indulge the belief that they *cannot* govern, that it is impossible for them to secure proper order, they may as well *tell* their feelings to the whole school; the scholars will not be slow to read their thoughts, and will " govern themselves accordingly."

It is not my design to say that all have equal ability to govern, or that the object is accomplished when the teacher has made the decided *resolve* to be obeyed; but I do say that teachers cannot exercise a proper and uniform authority, any longer than they *believe* they can do so. This is a natural principle. When we believe we can obtain a desired object, we try, but when we think we cannot, our efforts are feeble. The next direction in regard to government is, *consider your scholars as intelligent and reasonable beings.* As such, they will be influenced by motives, when properly presented. They may easily be brought to know that they are happier when they do right than when they do wrong. And when the right and the wrong are both placed distinctly before them, they will seldom call the wrong object the right, or the reverse. Right and wrong may be exhibited before the mind of a child of few years. This appeal will usually exert a far better influence upon him, in leading him to duty, than any other mode. I shall be better understood in what I wish to say on this point by an example.

A complaint was made to the instructor, by George, against John, who was accused of having struck and otherwise injured his school-fellow. After ascertaining the facts, and finding that the complaint was well founded, a course like the following was pursued.

Instructor. John, I am sorry to find a complaint of this kind brought against you. You have been so unwise as to make yourself unhappy, and to make others unhappy also. You may stand up and answer some questions which I wish to propose. Is it right for one scholar to beat or abuse another?

John. No, sir.

Inst. Do you think that the school could make good progress in study, if all the scholars should treat each other as you have treated George?

John. I think not.

Inst. Are you willing that one of the larger boys should beat you, or otherwise abuse you?

John. No, sir.

Inst. Do you think it is right for you to do to others as you are unwilling they should do to you?

John. I do not think it is.

[Such answers would be almost invariably given, under similar circumstances. Not one child in a thousand would give those different, where the teacher commences with him in a deliberate and gentle manner. Conscience assures him he has done wrong; and one must be uncommonly hardened, who would say that he had done right. If he be inclined to excuse himself, because George said or did something that displeased him, he should be shown that he is accountable for his *own* conduct, and that misbehavior in another person does not alter the nature of his own sin. That the offence of one does not justify a far greater error in another, may be shown by reference to any judicial proceeding.]

The teacher proceeded: When one scholar injures another, ought he to make satisfaction for it?

John. I suppose he ought.

Inst. Well, do you think you ought to make any satisfaction to George?

John. I don't know but I ought.

Inst. I wish you to give me a specific answer. Is it right or wrong for you to make satisfaction?

John. It is right.

Inst. Are you willing to do right, when you know what is right?

John. [After some hesitation.] Yes, sir.

Inst. Are you willing, then, to go to George, and make satisfaction?

[Here John hesitated again; but after the question had been repeated, said that he was. In pursuing a mode similar to this, a great many times, I have scarcely found an instance where the culprit has not said he was willing to make satisfaction to the injured party. In the case described, John was directed to inquire of George what would be satisfactory; George promptly replied, "Say he is sorry, and promise not to do so any more."]

The teacher then remarked: You have done what is right in regard to George, but that does not make satisfaction to others who have been injured. You have set a very bad example, have broken the rules of the school, and have caused the loss of time, which might have been improved in gaining knowledge. Is it not right, therefore, that I should require satisfaction in behalf of the school?

John. I suppose it is.

Inst. Yes, it is right that every offence should be suitably atoned for. And this must be complied with in your case. I have not, however, reflected on the subject sufficiently, and shall defer it till two o'clock to-morrow, and shall attend to it precisely at the time appointed. I hope you will yourself reflect much on the subject, and be able to tell me what is right for me to require.

It has ever appeared to me, that punishment,

if it become necessary in any case, should *be deferred for a season.* But precisely at the time set, it should be attended to. By deferring the subject, as in the case above mentioned, the pupil has opportunity to reflect. He is induced to reflect on the nature of his offence, that he may form an idea of the punishment he shall probably receive. Such reflection will be of more service to him than any severity of punishment whatever. Indeed, I have seldom been obliged to call a scholar to account more than once, where I have pursued a course like that above described.

I will suppose another case, to illustrate the direction to treat the scholars as moral and intellectual beings.

Laura came to the instructor and wished to be excused from writing a composition, which had been required of her. The instructor inquired: Why do you wish me to excuse you, Laura?

Laura. I don't know what to write; I cannot write anything fit to be seen.

Inst. Well, Laura, we will converse about it. Do you wish to be excused from spelling, reading, or writing.

Laura. No, sir.

Inst. Why not from these as well as from writing a composition?

Laura. They are easy; and, besides, we could not do without a knowledge of them.

Inst. Could you always read, Laura?

Laura. No, sir.

Inst. How is it that you can read now?

Laura. I have *learned* how to read.

Inst. How long were you in trying to learn, before you could read with ease?

Laura. I do not know, it was a long time.

Inst. Did you tell the teacher that you wished to be excused, and that you never could learn, and that you could not read in a way "fit to be" heard?

Laura. No, I did not. [*Smiling.*]

Inst. I saw you knitting and sewing the other day: could you always knit and sew?

Laura. I could not.

Inst. How, then, can you do so now?

Laura. Because, I have learned how to do both.

Inst. How did you learn?

Laura. By trying.

Inst. Did you ever tell your mother she must excuse you from knitting and sewing, because you did not know how, and could not sew or knit fit to be seen?

Laura. I did not.

Inst. Why did you not?

Laura. I knew if I did not keep trying, I never could learn, and so I kept on.

Inst. Do you think it is necessary to know how to write letters, and to express ourselves properly when writing?

Laura. O yes, sir.

Inst. You expect to have occasion to write letters, do you not?

Laura. I presume I shall, for I have written to my brother and cousin already.

Inst. Then you think, if I should aid you in learning to write a letter or other piece of composition *properly*, that I should do you a great benefit.

Laura. I suppose, sir, you would.

Inst. Is it right for me to benefit you and the school as much as I can?

Laura. I suppose, sir, you ought to aid us all you can.

Inst. Should I do right, if I neglect the means which will benefit you?

Laura. No, sir.

Inst. Now I will answer you. You asked if I would excuse you from writing? I will do so, if you think I could be justified in neglecting to benefit you as much as I can. If you can say sincerely, that you believe it is my duty to do wrong to the school, by indulging them in neglecting what they ought to learn, then I will comply with your request.

Laura frankly acknowledged that the teacher ought not to excuse her from this exercise.

By a course like the above, the scholar is led to see that you act on principle; that you wish the best good of those committed to your care. The child whom you treat in this way will be led to reflection, and will inquire what views the instructor will take on a subject before he concludes to come to you with a request. As far as practicable, explain to the school the reason of everything you do. Let them know that you regard their good in all the regulations made. Explain to them the reason why one thing is right and another wrong, and they will generally understand you, and will be governed far more easily than by resorting to the whip and ferule. In no way can you so readily conciliate the willing obedience of your scholars, as by pursuing such a course; and in no way can you sooner make them your enemies, than by treating them as if incapable of being controlled by any principle but fear. Reason should be equally your guide in making rules and in executing them; in granting the requests of your scholars and refusing them. First, ask yourself, is the request a reasonable one? and after using proper means to ascertain, and taking time to decide judiciously, let the decision be such as duty requires. You may not always be able to decide at the moment; if not, take time, remembering that *no decision at all* is preferable to a *wrong one;* and while the scholar is waiting to know the opinion you entertain, he will generally be led to reflect on the principles by which you will be governed, and will commonly be prepared to submit cheerfully to your decision.

The next direction on the subject of government is, *let it be uniform.* Many fail on this point. I am willing to confess it is very difficult to be so, while the health and spirits of most persons fluctuate so much. But still, uniformity is indispensable. I have seen some instructors very strict one day, and very indulgent the next. I have myself been reproved and punished for doing that which at some previous time had appeared to please the teacher. To approve to-day what you condemn to-morrow, is certainly very injudicious. But to something of this, all teachers are in more or less danger, from the different states of temper and spirits in which they find themselves. We can bear fatigue at some times better than at others. When suffering under a headache, a school may appear to us very noisy, which at another time would appear very still, so different are the states of the nervous system at different times.

Another fault exists in many schools. The small scholars are strictly governed, while the larger do nearly as they please. I have often seen the child of six years punished severely for a fault, that was hardly noticed when committed by a young man of eighteen. This is unreasonable; it is *wicked.* If there should be any difference in the treatment of the two cases, it should be reversed. If a necessary rule is violated by an older scholar, the wrong is greater than when the same rule is disregarded by one younger. The former deserves severer rebuke or punishment, for he is better able to comprehend the rules of propriety. The older scholars should never be suffered to transgress with impunity laws which you have made for the government of the whole school. They will respect you the less for indulging them in what is improper, and will show a growing disregard for your feelings and for your authority.

Do you say the oldest scholars are able to govern themselves, and that your business is only with the younger ones? True, those who have arrived at years of manhood, *ought* to govern themselves; but they must be different from the great mass of youth, not to need admonition or restraint. When it becomes necessary to establish a rule in the school, see that it be regarded by all; and you will find your task much easier and will gain the confidence of the school much more than by the opposite course.

Be not only uniform, but *firm*. Let it be known as your established rule, that every reasonable requisition must be complied with by all, and you will find it more easy to secure implicit obedience. If a scholar ask of you some indulgence, be sure to examine its propriety before you say no or yes to his request. But when you have decided, adhere to this answer. To deny the request of a scholar when it is first made, and then, in a few minutes, grant what he desires, because he continues asking, is certainly injudicious. If he give a good reason for repeating his request, you may change your decision; but the reason ought to be assigned at first, and then the answer given with reference to it be final.

I have not unfrequently visited schools, where, if a scholar asked leave to go out, the answer was perhaps instantly given, "No; sit down." Within a minute the request was repeated; the answer again was, "No." But after the question had been repeated half a dozen times, the patience of the teacher seemed to be exhausted, and he replied, "Yes, yes; I had rather you would go, than to keep asking all the time." Now the impression was left, doubtless, on the mind of that scholar, that the teacher had less regard to what was right or wrong in the case, than he had to his own convenience. Scholars must have considered the teacher as fickle in mind, and respect for him must have been diminished.

The instructor, harassed by the many questions asked during the day, is in danger of forming the habit of answering them without due consideration, and merely to be rid of them. But this, if ever practised, is very censurable. Let the members of every school be taught to expect the teachers will abide by the decision they make in every case, and that such decisions are made in view of all the circumstances. By a different course, scholars will very soon learn to disregard what you say, disbelieve your promises, and neglect your commands. I will only add that without firmness of purpose in the government of a school, it will be impossible to make that school pleasant to the teacher or profitable to the pupil.

Let the government of the school be impartial. In this direction, I do not wish to imply that you are to exercise the same feelings towards every individual. Good instructors will love, and ought to love, the good scholar more than the bad. They cannot, and will not, feel an equal regard for the obedient and the disobedient, for the docile and the perverse. But, notwithstanding this, teachers should be impartial to all. Though you cannot love an idle, heedless, unmannerly child, so much as the affectionate, studious, and obedient one; yet if, when the good scholar commits a fault, you neglect to call him to account for it, and punish a less agreeable scholar for a similar offence, the latter will accuse you of injustice, and with good reason. For if you have made a law, it is for the whole school, and should be regarded by all. No complaint is more frequently heard, than that the instructor is partial, and treats one better than another, etc. It will be no matter for wonder if this charge is sometimes unjustly made. But I am constrained to say that, without great care, instructors *may* be betrayed into a greater or less degree of it, almost every day. There may, indeed, be sometimes a propriety in making a difference in the treatment of the same fault under different circumstances. The same law may be broken by two persons, and very different degrees of criminality be attached to each. The man who passes you a counterfeit dollar *ignorantly*, breaks the letter of the law, as much as the knave who passes it knowingly. But the first is guilty of no intentional fraud. One scholar may transgress a reasonable rule of the school, and may have been led to it by the persuasion of those older or better informed than himself; while another may be guilty of the same offence, without any palliating circumstances. There may be a propriety in treating them very differently, and in so doing you need not be guilty of partiality. When the circumstances are the same, the treatment shonld be uniform. Partiality, if exhibited in your treatment of scholars, will deprive you of their confidence. Children are not slow to discover it where it exists, and when they believe that any one of their number may do wrong and go unpunished, while another will be treated with severity for the same offence, it is impossible to exert any useful influence over them. There is a loss to them, and much inconvenience to the teacher; and not only this, but he is guilty of doing wrong, and must suffer the rebuke of his own conscience.

Avoid everything, in the government of a school, which has a tendency to produce the impression on the minds of the young, that the laws under which they are placed are barriers to their true happiness. All wise laws are designed to secure the welfare of those who are subject to them. The laws of Jehovah all originate in infinite wisdom and infinite love. A good writer* remarks: "God's laws will not be altered for our accommodation. We may obey them, or disobey them; see them, or not see them; we may be wise, or unwise; but they will be rigidly and unalterably enforced. Thus must it ever be. By obedience to the laws of God, man may be as happy as his present state will allow. But misery, sooner or later, will inevitably follow disobedience. Hence, our great business here is to know and obey the laws of our glorious Creator."

It cannot be asserted, I know, that all *human*

---

* Dr. Wayland.

laws are adapted to secure the *highest happiness* of those for whom they are designed; for through passion, pride, and prejudice, laws may be made by those, to whom a law-making power is delegated, that are wrong, are in opposition to the laws of God. Such laws may exist. But, is it saying more than the truth, that, in our own land, the laws of society, in general, are established in *wisdom*, and *cannot be violated with impunity?* They are not *intended* to endanger our safety, invade our rights, or defeat our enjoyment, but to secure them all. So far as founded in reason, so far as they are derived from the laws of our Maker, if obeyed, they must, they will, secure both safety and happiness.

Whenever modes of discipline are adopted in a family or school, that have a tendency to lead its subjects to the belief that the laws under which they are necessarily placed are cruel, — are opposed to their safety and enjoyment, — discipline fails of its end. For, human nature being what it is, there will be efforts, either secretly to *evade* law and authority, or openly to *trample* them under foot.

Adopt that mode of government which will most naturally lead the young to the practice of self-government. I would not be understood to imply that the sole object of school discipline, should be to cherish habits of self-government. It should, undoubtedly, secure the present good and convenience of teacher and pupil. But this falls short of accomplishing *all* the ends of discipline. As the knowledge communicated is not for the present so much as the future good of the young, so the government exercised over them should relate to the future as well as the present. Each one, at a certain age, is expected to be left to his own discretion, to govern himself. The earlier he is prepared for this, the better he is qualified for enjoyment; and the more secure are the foundations for happiness to him. To qualify children to do this, should, therefore, be a prominent object in the discipline of schools; this being one of the greatest blessings teachers can confer on their pupils. If the teacher so holds the reins, that his pupils are moved by his *presence* only to do right; if they are never allowed to try their own pinions, to attempt self-government, to feel responsibility; or, in other words, to practise self-government; they can certainly cherish but little confidence in their ability, whether they possess it or not. That kind of discipline, or supervision, over the young, which leads them to regard merely the question, whether they shall be punished or not, for any particular course of conduct, or to inquire only whether the teacher will be pleased or displeased, and not whether the course of conduct is *right* or *wrong*, is, most obviously, far from being likely to secure the best results of judicious discipline. If I may be allowed to express my personal conviction, with regard to the *more common* defects in school discipline, I must say that I regard this as one of them.

What proportion of those, placed at the head

of schools, of one grade and another, make it a prominent object to teach their pupils the art of self-government? Is not the proportion, admitting the confessions of teachers themselves as evidence, very small? And can any one doubt, that one of the greatest favors which you can confer on a child, is to teach him *how* to govern himself, and lead him to do it?

Do you ask how this is to be done? I reply, in short, make the scholar acquainted with the true character of law, with its value and tendency. Point out to him the various relations he sustains to his fellows, and his Maker; explain to him the responsibilities under which he acts; make him acquainted with the true nature of both happiness and misery; with the way in which one is to be secured, and the other averted; and, above all, lead him to act in view of the inevitable consequences of his own conduct, and you will have, in some measure at least, accomplished your object.

In this place, allow me to present several somewhat miscellaneous suggestions. In all your arrangements and plans for the government of your schools, consult not only your own convenience and the *present* welfare of the scholars, but pursue such a course as shall produce the most permanently beneficial results. To do this, the instructor must be *master*, in all places and at all hours. It is not enough that you govern and restrain your scholars during school hours, but you must regard their conduct at all other times when they are not under the care of their parents. I have sometimes been acquainted with instructors, who seemed to notice the behavior of their pupils only while they were in school. By a proper course, teachers may as easily direct the amusement and play of their scholars as their studies, and it is hardly less important that they should do so. For this purpose they should show an interest in their sports, and a willingness that they should amuse themselves during the usual intermissions of study. The difference between various kinds of exercise should be indeed carefully pointed out, and such as are injurious should be prohibited. Amusements that corrupt the morals or the taste, and such as have a tendency to injure the health or limbs, should be discountenanced. Also, such exercises as tend to excite jealousies and hatred, or to interest the mind so much as to divert it from books and study, together with all the games of hazard and chance, are certainly prejudicial, and should be forbidden. Many of them prevent progress in study, and all of them are injurious to the morals of the scholars. In those districts where the male and female members continue at the school-room during intermission, the subject of proper exercise requires much more attention than in villages where they return home. Every exercise that is immodest or unbecoming should be prohibited, and whatever would give offence to the most delicate minds, of either sex, cannot be approved.

In order to be able to exercise this full and

judicious control, it will be very important that the school should know what you approve and what you disapprove, and the reasons on which your opinion is founded. Exercise or play proper in one school, may be impracticable or inexpedient in another. There may be circumstances that will have a very important influence in directing your recommendations of amusements and exercise. It should be your object to examine what may be attended with the fewest evils and the greatest good, and give advice accordingly.

There is another point on which I wish to remark. It relates to *the manner of speaking* proper in school, both for teacher and pupil. It will generally be found true, that the mode of address adopted by the teacher in speaking to the scholars, will be copied by them in addressing each other. Everything dictatorial, lordly, and austere, should be avoided. A spirit of affection should be infused into the whole school. Ask a scholar to do what you desire, in just such a tone as you would naturally use in asking a favor of a superior. Never command, unless the pupil has neglected to do as you requested him. To display your authority before there is any encroachment upon it, or any disposition shown to disregard it, is not needful. Perhaps there is no way, in which children may be led to speak kindly and affectionately to each other, so easily, as by the example of the teacher in speaking kindly and affectionately to them. And if any suppose that they are adding to their dignity and importance, in the estimation of their scholars, by assuming airs of great superiority or lordliness, such persons must have very little knowledge of human nature. President Monroe lost none of his dignity, when, during his tour to New England, he cordially took even children by the hand, and spoke kindly and affectionately to them.

When it is necessary to call a scholar to account for improper conduct, the same affectionate manner is recommended. I would much rather say to a child whom I saw breaking some important rule of school, "John, you may come to me," than to say, "Come here, John." The more benevolent, kind, and affectionate you are, the more plainly will he see the impropriety of breaking those laws which are designed by you for his benefit.

In this connection, it will be expected, perhaps, that I say something on the subject of punishments; for, after the greatest fidelity and discretion on the part of the instructor, there may be some who will not yield a reasonable and cheerful obedience. Such must be punished, both for their own reformation and as a warning to others. It would be doing injustice to those who are well disposed, to suffer the bad, by their frequent misconduct, to prevent them from making the progress they desire.

I have already supposed a case, where a scholar was found guilty of doing wrong, and have pointed out the way in which I would proceed in that particular case. To the suggestions before made under another head, I would here add a very few general directions.

Never make remarks implying that you *expect scholars will do wrong;* and be not in haste to accuse them. If *not* guilty, the child feels grieved that you should suppose him to have done wrong. After having been wrongfully accused, he will probably have less dread of doing wrong than before; for he already feels in some measure degraded, in having been supposed guilty. It is a principle in the civil law, "to suppose every man innocent till he is found guilty." In every case, an inquiry for evidence of the fact, ought to precede our accusation. To make inquiry for the evidence to prove the *innocence* of a scholar, may often be attended with happy consequences. If acquitted by the evidence adduced in his favor, he will love his teacher the better for having pursued this course; and if proved guilty, he will be more likely to be affected by what you may say to him afterwards.

Be not *in haste to punish* after a fault has been committed. Your first object should be, to converse with the scholar, to show him the nature of his crime, and to convince him that he has done that which, if others followed his example, would destroy the usefulness of the school. If his crime be that of profaneness, lying, or anything in direct violation of the laws of God, to those all-wise laws he should be referred. The awful consequences of these vices to himself, should be expressly shown. Their effect on the school, if others should follow his example, and their effect on every community, if all should be guilty of them, ought clearly to be exhibited. After this, he may be required to commit to memory those passages in the sacred Scripture, which show with what abhorrence the Supreme Being looks upon those enormities. When he has had sufficient time to reflect on the subject, he will be in a state to be profited by proper punishment. I would recommend to you never to punish for an offence the same day on which it was committed. The scholar will usually endeavor to forget the subject when the punishment is over; but he cannot, when he knows it is to come. It may, at times, be proper to defer it for two or three days, or a week. Whenever the time arrives, it should, as before intimated, receive attention, to the exclusion of everything else. Before being punished, he should be interrogated concerning the degree of punishment which he thinks his crime deserves, and if he appears to view his offence as more trifling than he ought, it is important to make him sensible, if possible, of his error. If you *must* punish, do it with seriousness. To exhibit any levity, to laugh, while you are inflicting punishment, must always be attended with bad consequences. The sufferer cannot feel otherwise than indignant. He will have good reason to accuse you of a wanton delight in his suffering, rather than of having a desire to do him good. Decide on such a mode as will be most likely to benefit the scholar, and *prevent a repetition* of the crime. Those punishments which have an effect on the body only, usually do little to prevent crime or to reclaim the guilty. As far as possible, strive to have it a punishment that will affect the mind rather than the body. To require the delinquent to ask forgiveness of the instructor, or of the school, — sometimes to require him to read a written confession to the school, or to parents, or guardians, — will have the desired effect. Much must be left to the judgment of the teacher at the time. Punishment should be varied with the disposition, age, or circumstances of the scholar, or the nature of his offence. It is undoubtedly true, that corporeal punishment should be the last resort. When everything else fails, you may have recourse to that. It is sometimes necessary, it sometimes does good. But yet, I am fully persuaded it is seldom necessary. Where a reasonable, calm, and decided course is adopted, where an instructor makes an appeal to the moral sensibility of the child, and shows him the nature of his fault, experience has satisfied me, that recourse to it will not be necessary, except in those cases where the child seems devoid of common sensibility, or where he has been neglected till his passions are too strong to be controlled by his reason.

Always make the punishment *effectual.* This rule is important, whether the punishment be of one kind or another. If the child deserves the punishment, it should not pass off till he is brought to feel it as such, and to realize the nature of the crime which he has committed. It is sometimes true, that a child punished but slightly is only injured, not benefited. He boasts that his chastisement did not hurt him, that he does not care, and sometimes that he loves to be punished. Now if the subject passes off in such a way, it would have been better, probably, to have neglected punishment entirely. His chastisement does him no good, if it does not humble him, and cause him to fear being brought again under the censure of his instructor.

Connected with punishments is the subject of rewards. These may sometimes be beneficial; but, as they are usually bestowed, they probably do as much harm as good. To promise a reward, is often an excitement to study for the sake of the reward; not as a duty, or from a love of learning, or a desire to merit the approbation of the wise and good.

When a prize is offered to a number of competitors, those who hope to gain it will be excited to emulation and to envy; and those who have no such hope will usually be discouraged, and probably make less progress than if no reward had been offered. I would advise you to *promise* no rewards, and if you ever give them, let such honors be grounded on the excellence of the scholar, his industry and faithfulness, rather than the amount of knowledge he obtains in a given time. One scholar may require a week to learn what another will accomplish in a day. If the former perseveres and is faithful in his slow and toilsome progress, he is to be commended rather than the other; for he has greater obstacles to encounter, and has succeeded in overcoming them.

It is not impossible but he may be the more benefited of the two. For it is commonly true that those who learn very easily forget as easily, while those who learn slowly remember better what they have acquired. It is not unusual for the slow gains of the mechanic to be eventually more productive than the rapid and golden streams of the merchant.

If rewards are given at all, let them be "rewards of *merit*," and not rewards for mere intellectual capacity. The dull of apprehension are not to be punished for being so, neither do the more gifted merit praise for what they have received from the hand of God.

LECTURE VIII.

YOUNG LADIES AND GENTLEMEN: —

IN connection with the government, I wish to direct your attention to the *general management of schools*. This is a subject of much consequence; for though you may be able to govern with ease, yet it is possible that you may fail, by ill-directed effort, of accomplishing all that is reasonably expected of you. Though you must fail in everything *without good government*, yet government alone will not accomplish *all* the objects you ought to have in view.

In the general management of a school, it is important to keep in mind always, that the great object is to prepare children to be happy; to be useful to themselves and others; and to teach them how to *acquire* knowledge and how to *apply* it. In a word, the purpose of education is to teach how to think and how to act right in all the vicissitudes of life. The general management of a school, then, must be decided by a reference to these objects. It should regard both the present enjoyment and the future good of its members. Let me say to every teacher: —

1. Endeavor to adopt such a course as shall render the school *pleasant*. If children associate study with a variety of agreeable objects, they will be led to think of it as a pleasure. We are all much affected by the objects around us: if they are pleasant, we are pleased; if gloomy or disgusting, it is hardly possible for us to be cheerful and happy. If we see others smile or weep, we are disposed to do the same. Let the teacher of the school wear a smiling countenance, let him appear happy, and desirous of making others so, and he will hardly fail of seeing smiling faces and contented looks around him.

Instructors do not always appreciate the great importance of having a school-room kept neat, and of requiring the books and all the apparatus of the school to be arranged in the best order. I commend warmly the practice of a teacher whose school I once visited. Over the door was a card, with the words "ORDER, NEATNESS,

PROMPTNESS, *and* THOROUGHNESS, *essential prerequisites to a good school.*" At the commencement of school, after ringing a bell, she inquired, "Are we ready to begin? Is everything in place, and ready for use?" and as soon as every hand was raised, she remarked, "the exercises may commence." Before dismissing, she insisted that every book, slate, etc., should be carefully put in their appropriate places; and she never dismissed school till the signal was given by all, that everything was in order. Nothing was allowed to be out of place during any part of the day, and no litter to accumulate around any desk. Equal pains were taken to have as many pleasing objects as possible placed in the school-room. Maps, pictures, and paintings were beautifully arranged on the walls. These and similar efforts, cost but little time, but added greatly to the pleasantness of the school. On a card back of the teacher's desk were the words: *A time for everything, and everything in its time.*" Let all teachers imitate her example.

2. Reduce everything to system. This will have a great tendency to promote what is required in the previous advice. By means of system, much more can be accomplished than is possible without it. Irregularity is the enemy of happiness, and where it extensively prevails it entirely prevents success in any business. By having a time for everything, and doing everything in its season, you will be enabled to avoid confusion, to know what to do, and to take pleasure in doing it.

But if you wait for the subjects to present themselves before you think what to do, twenty things may sometimes come up at once, and, in your perplexity to choose among them, you are unprepared to attend to any. He who tries to do many things at once, will accomplish nothing. "He that has many irons in the fire, must let some of them burn," says an *old* but true proverb.

In order to introduce system, *attempt to do only one thing at a time.* The opposite of this I have frequently seen.

An instructor called a class to read, and in a moment a scholar wished for a copy; the master neglected his class, and prepared to set one; while doing that, a boy came with a pen to be mended, and before this was done another wished to be assisted in his arithmetic. While mending the pen and looking at the slate, another came and wished to be shown some place on the atlas; the pen and slate were neglected, and the copy and the class, and two or three minutes were devoted to finding the place on the map. Several other calls were now made at once, and the teacher neglected all the former to scold the latter for making him so much trouble. Here were ten or twelve scholars all waiting, all doing nothing, excepting the *class*, which had kept on reading, pronouncing half the words wrong, and neglecting every rule which would have rendered the exercise useful. They were then told they had read enough, and that they might sit down. The other matters were despatched after a while;

another class was called to read, and a similar course was pursued. Now how in the name of common sense can a teacher endure this? what benefit can the scholar derive? The teacher had no plan, no system, no order; hence, he could not avoid confusion and perplexity. In all sorts of business system is important, but in schools it is indispensable, if the happiness of either teacher or pupil is sought. While a class is reading, the entire attention of the teacher should be given to that exercise. He will thus be able to give useful instructions. When a class is called to spell, let this receive the entire attention. The same should be observed in regard to writing, grammar, arithmetic, geography, etc. In this way, everything will be done without confusion. But by having no system, much must be neglected that should receive attention, and that be but imperfectly done which is attempted to be accomplished.

3. Another direction is, let everything be done *thoroughly* when commenced. It may be said, perhaps, that there is not time; that if the school is large, it is impossible to go through with the required exercises thoroughly. Now if this be true, I still insist on the direction to do everything thoroughly, when it is commenced. If a subject can receive attention but once a day, or but once in two days, the scholar will derive more advantage from one lesson in two days, if well recited and properly explained, than from half a dozen, if but half recited and not explained. In teaching, as in other matters, the old adage is true, "Work once well done is twice done."

4. Let subjects be classed according to their importance, and each receive proportionate attention. Some instructors have been known to spend a large part of their time in teaching a small class who were pursuing a favorite branch. In this manner, studies vastly important to the majority of scholars have received very little attention. If the teacher is much better pleased with grammar than with arithmetic, and has a class of five in that, while there are fifteen in this, he does great injury to the latter, if he spends double the time with the smaller class. And yet, if more fond of teaching grammar than arithmetic, the teacher is in danger of doing so. Those subjects which we have most frequently occasion to use, are more important to us than those which we seldom wish to employ.

Reading and spelling are more important than geography, because without an acquaintance with the former, we are deprived of the means of knowledge. We have occasion to employ our knowledge of reading much more frequently than a knowledge of geography. So arithmetic is more important than grammar, because we find occasion to use it in the business of life much oftener than we do the rules of syntax, to which we attend at school. The instructor should endeavor to divide time, so as to give to each particular subject that degree of attention which properly belongs to it. It is manifestly wrong to give an undue portion of time to some one subject, merely because he may have higher taste for it than for some other.

The *direction of studies* will claim much attention. The best rule I can give on this point is, to follow the order of nature. Let those studies receive attention first which may be most easily understood and comprehended by children ; and then let others follow in the order which common sense would dictate. It would no doubt be impracticable to attempt to introduce fully, in our schools, the German or Prussian method entire. In those schools, during the first and second year that children attend, oral instruction *only* is given. During this period, children are taught the elements of natural history ; the elements of arithmetic ; are taught to sing, and also to observe and describe all familiar objects ; in which exercise, constant attention is paid to accuracy in pronunciation and the use of words ; they thus acquire the elements of grammar, without the name. The accuracy with which children in those schools speak, and describe objects, before they are seven years of age, would be surprising to the best instructors in this country. But though it may be impracticable to attempt to introduce the German method fully, some parts may be copied. Oral instruction is of great importance, preceding the period when children are able to employ books in getting lessons. Hints, however, on this subject will be given when discussing the mode of teaching.

When the child has acquired so much knowledge of reading as to be able to give a proper pronunciation to syllables and words, his attention should be directed to their *meaning*. Words are signs of ideas; and it is an object of high importance that a very early habit should be formed, of ascertaining their meaning. Not being able to have recourse to a dictionary, it must devolve on the teacher to explain words. This should, as much as possible, be done by means of sensible objects. Some little story in which the word occurs may be related to a child, which will often fix the meaning permanently in his mind; or the word may be explained by its opposite. Much attention should be given at this time to pronunciation. This will be learned mostly from the example of the teacher. Great care is necessary here, because it is as easy to learn right as wrong at first, and when one has been taught wrong, it requires more time to unlearn than to learn right at first.

Children are capable at a very early age of understanding something of numbers. They can be taught to enumerate and to read figures much earlier than many suppose, as has been proved in infant schools. They may be taught to add, subtract, multiply, and divide, by the aid of tangible or visible objects. By this process they will be able to form distinct ideas of the nature and combination of numbers. I would not be understood to imply, that children at a very early age will be able to comprehend the more complex operations of arithmetic, but the simple rules are easily made intelligible to children from four to six years of age.

Geography may be an early study. Having a picture or map before him, the child will be able to understand what he could not without such occular demonstration. Children are almost always pleased with maps. Hence they are interested in this study at an age when it would be impossible to engage their attention in the exercise without the aid of maps.

History may be an early study with children. They are commonly pleased with stories, and where the terms made use of in little histories are such as they can comprehend, and the facts in the narrative are prominent, they will be interested and amused. It is desirable that the geography and history first used should be of one's own town, State, or country.

After some attention has been paid to these subjects, the scholar will be prepared to attend profitably to arithmetic and geography in a more thorough manner, and to pursue those parts which would not at first have been intelligible or interesting.

Grammar may, in its most simple parts, be early understood and rendered interesting. But the child requires judgment, to be able to apply the rules of syntax. After some knowledge of these branches has been gained, it is not so important what others shall follow them. It will be important, however, to have regard constantly to the probable destination of the child. To direct the preparatory studies of a merchant or mechanic in the same manner as of a teacher or physician, is not always judicious. Some ground is, indeed, common to all. But particular branches may essentially benefit one, which may be dispensed with by another, without serious disadvantage.

The general management of a school has necessarily intimate relation to the *mode* of *imparting instruction.* As I address those who will conduct summer schools, as well as those who will be employed in schools taught in winter, before proceeding to the general suggestions on the mode of teaching, I will offer a few remarks having more special reference to schools where the pupils are young. Many schools of this class are constituted principally of children under eight years of age. In such schools much time must be spent in oral instruction, or the pupils can derive but little benefit. The exercises may, and ought to be, conducted differently from schools where the larger part can use books, and prepare regular lessons. I can present no hints to teachers in such schools which will be more valuable than those taken in part from a description of one of the schools in Hartford, Connecticut, as given by the conductors of the Journal of Education, several years ago:—

"I have before remarked, that an object of the first importance is, to teach children to *think;* to call into exercise their own powers of mind. For this purpose, various means may be used. The teacher will be obliged to tax her invention from day to day, and to vary her course according to the circumstances in which she is placed. An eminent instructor observed, a few years since, that, after all our improvements, there was still one sort of schools wanted, namely, *thinking schools*. Every school, however, where the pupils are taught rationally, is in effect a thinking school. Formerly, many teachers seemed to suppose their whole duty consisted in filling children's heads with words. The child who could commit the greatest number of verses or pages to memory in a given time, was considered the best scholar. For this erroneous practice, another has recently been substituted, which is scarcely less pernicious. Finding that words did not always convey ideas, and justly supposing it important to make everything presented to children perfectly intelligible, — instead of words to give them ideas, — it was hence hastily concluded that they would be learned in proportion to the *number* of ideas which could be crowded into their minds. This is a great mistake. As well might it be supposed that the physical frame of a child will grow exactly in proportion to the quantity of food which can be crammed into his stomach, as that the mind expands in exact proportion to the number of ideas or facts with which it is crowded. Nothing nourishes or gives vigor in either case, but what is, in a certain sense at least, digested. In both cases, more at a time than can be digested is not only useless but injurious

" Considerable pains is taken here to make the children *think ;* though not half as much as is desirable. There is still too much filling the mind with the ideas of others, instead of habituating the pupil to teach himself, and make those ideas his own. In order to have ideas *our own*, we must be led to originate them, as it were, for ourselves; we must learn how to arrange them, and when and where to apply them. A person might have the best *chest of tools* in the world, but would he therefore *of course* be a mechanic?

"The familiar, common sense explanations and illustrations of science, which are given here from day to day, have a wonderful effect, so far as they go, in teaching the pupils to think, and invent, and originate for themselves. The following plan is sometimes adopted, both to teach them to think, and as a physical exercise: —

"They are requested in the first place to sit still a few minutes, and try to recall some fact of which they have heard or read; or recollect something which has fallen within the range of their own observation. After a short interval of silence, those who have thought of something to say, raise their hands. The teacher then selects one from this number, who goes to the middle of the floor, and repeats, in a distinct voice, the fact which he has thought of. Sometimes, they walk once round the room while they are speaking. The pupil then takes his seat, and another follows in the same manner. They are very fond of this exercise, and I never saw them weary of it; but they always leave it off with apparent reluctance. Indeed, it should be so; for then they will enter upon it in future with the same eagerness as before.

"Great pains is taken to render these little

speeches the results of their own mental operations. They are not often suffered to repeat the precise language they have read or heard, but are required to invent language of their own. They are, however, constantly falling into this habit of imitation, unless they are guarded. To ascertain whether they understand the words they use, they are frequently questioned on the subject.

"An experienced instructor in this State used to require her oldest class of pupils to recall, and be able to relate, every morning, the events and exercises of the preceding day. The time assigned to this exercise was immediately after reading in the New Testament, at the opening of the school. They were required to think closely for ten minutes, the teacher informing them when the time was expired. After this, any one of them was liable to be called upon to give the narration. Some of them used to relate everything in the most minute manner."

Another mode may be successfully adopted. The teacher, holding in her hands some object, suppose a fragment of stone, asks, —

Children, do you see what I have in my hand?

C. Nothing but a piece of stone.

T. Well, what do you suppose I am going to do with it; can you think?

1st C. I don't know.

2d C. Talk to us about it.

3d C. Tell us to *think* about it.

T. Can any of you think of anything to say about it. [A pause.]

T. Who made it?

C. God made it; for he made everything.

T. Did he make it for any purpose?

C. He did; for nothing is made in vain.

T. Can you think of any use to which stones are applied? Each one who can think of anything, may tell me.

1*st C.* To make walls.

2*d C.* To make doorsteps.

3*d C.* Houses are underpinned with stones.

4*th C.* Do not people pave streets with stones?

5*th C.* I have seen a *house* made of stones.

T. Anything else? *think.*

C. Millstones, to grind corn and wheat with.

2*d. C.* I went over a bridge once that was made of stones.

T. Can any one think of anything else?

C. Hearths are sometimes made of stones.

2*d C.* Jambs are also made of marble, which is one kind of stone.

T. Who can think of anything else for which stones are useful?

C. I remember of reading that Bunker Hill Monument is made of stone.

The teacher may ask the question several times; and when no one can think of any other use, she may explain the mode of obtaining lime from stone; the value of plaster-stone, as manure, etc.

At another time she holds up a nail, and asks, What is this, children?

C. A nail.

T. What is it made of?

C. Iron.

T. Can you tell me where iron comes from? Does it grow as trees do?

C. No; it is obtained from the ground.

T. Can you think of anything else that is made of iron?

C. Yes; a knife, a chain, an axe, a crane, a hoe, a part of ploughs and harrows.

T. Can you think of anything else?

C. Yes; the stove is made of iron.

T. Can you think of anything else?

C. Yes; a horseshoe.

T. Anything else?

When the teacher has elicited every answer that can be given by the children, she varies her questions, and inquires whether it is very useful; whether people could live in civilized society without it; or, whether iron or copper is the more useful. The conclusions they will be able to form will be very generally found correct. The chief benefit of this course is, the exercise of mind it gives to the children. They are led to think; to examine and inquire; and will thus be led to form habits of reflection.

A knife, book, pen, piece of glass, watch, flower, stick, etc., may be used in the same exercise, and the exercise will always receive attention. The course may be varied, by proposing questions like the following: —

Can any child mention anything that is great?

Why is —— great?

Who will mention something that is good?

Why is —— good ?

Mention something that is valuable ? Why is, —— valuable ?

Can you mention anything that is beautiful ? Why is it beautiful ?

Tell me of something that is mean, unkind, cowardly, wicked ; or virtuous, benevolent, lovely, praiseworthy, etc., etc.

In giving answers to these questions, a very young child will often discover reflection surprising to any one who has never performed the experiment. The teacher ought always to ask for the *reason* why the particular thing possesses the character ascribed to it by the child, and may remark as freely on every subject as may be considered necessary. If it is asked, how much time should be occupied in exercises of this character, I reply, that this must always be determined by circumstances. In a school where the children are nearly all able to pursue a regular study, and are prepared to improve time profitably in getting lessons, a much shorter portion of time should be thus employed than in other schools, where but few are able to read. In *every primary* school, however, some part of both the morning and afternoon ought to be thus occupied. If no more than five minutes can be spent in this way, it should be improved ; but fifteen or twenty minutes may in most cases be very usefully devoted, in each part of the day. An exercise in arithmetic, having the same object in view, has been conducted in many schools, with very great benefit to the children. I might easily spend the time of a whole Lecture in describing various modes in which you may proceed; but I will add the following only.

Take the numeral frame or arithmeticon; or, if not possessed of either of these, take pieces of paper, or anything else which may be seen by all the children at the same time; and, pointing to one at a time, let them count. Then change the exercise, and let them count by two and three, etc. As another exercise, they may be taught to add two to two, to four, to five, etc., continuing as far as they are able. Then add three to three, to four, etc. Exercises in subtracting, and the other fundamental rules, may be made equally simple; and children may, at a very early age, make some progress in them. Every teacher ought to have, as a guide in these exercises, arithmetical cards, or something similar.*

Another exercise by which habits of thinking can be promoted, may be, defining words. This may be done by giving a word, and requiring them to tell its opposite. The teacher may ask, What is the opposite to cold? The children will at once say, hot. What is the opposite of great, good, pretty, virtue, knowledge, etc.? I think this is one of the best means of leading children to distinct ideas of the knowledge of words, and it is always pleasing to them. Many other means may be employed for making them acquainted with words. One, that is well calculated to interest the

* Emerson's first No. of the N. A. Arithmetic may be usefully employed.

attention, is that of giving them a word to think of, and then reading a little story which will explain it. Let the word *cruelty* be given; then, to explain it, read the account of the treatment of Joseph by his brethren, and tell them that was *cruel*. The story of Absalom's usurping the throne of his father, and going to war with him, after his father had treated him with great kindness, will be a proper illustration. The story of the trial and scourging of the Saviour by the wicked Jews, will be perhaps a better illustration than either.

Another exercise may be in natural history. In this the youngest scholars may engage, and will always be found ready to give their attention. If not furnished with the infant school cards, every teacher should provide herself with as many pictures of animals, etc., as may be convenient. Whenever the children appear fatigued, they may, without any previous notice, be permitted to rise or gather round you while you proceed with a lesson. Many are furnished in the "Infant School Manual," which I hope every one employed in teaching very young children will possess. Much assistance may be derived from it.

A first lesson may be about the division, kinds, or classes, of animals. You may tell them the names of different classes and individuals, and also describe their most striking characteristics; as, quadrupeds, or four-footed; bipeds, or two-footed; carnivorous, or those that feed upon flesh, etc., etc. Fowls, fishes, serpents, insects, animalcule, etc., may be described. Trees may be divided into classes. Vegetables may also be classed; and those on which we depend for food and clothing may be particularly examined. But it will be better, generally, to defer a very particular attention to these, till after a number of lessons have been given on animals. The picture of a single animal may be sufficient to present at one time.

T. What animal does this picture represent?

C. A cow, [or as the case may be.]

T. Is the cow a quadruped or biped?

Is the cow carnivorous?

On what does she feed?

Where does the cow live?

Is she a valuable animal? why valuable?

Is she wild or tame? ferocious or gentle? large or small?

What does she furnish for our use?

What is the flesh of cows good for? what is it called?

Is the skin of any use? hair? horns? feet? bones?

Is any other part valuable?

Questions may be varied indefinitely, till everything is said which may be useful. The questions above may be easily altered, so as to be applicable to *any* animal of which you may have a picture.

The following Lessons are extracted from an interesting series, found in the "*Infant School Manual.*" I give them for the benefit of those who may not possess any book to aid them.

DEER.

What animal is this?

The deer.

How does it appear?

Very beautiful and harmless, and runs very swiftly.

For what is it useful?

The skin makes a soft and strong leather, which is made into gloves and shoes; their flesh makes delicious meat.

What is the meat called?

Venison. Its horns are useful in making knife-handles, and other articles. Butter and cheese are sometimes made of its milk.

To what age does it live?

Thirty-five or forty years.

What does the deer use for food?

It eats the stalks, leaves, and moss of trees.

What are the other animals of the deer kind called?

Fallow-deer, reindeer, roebuck, moose, and elk.

Where are all these animals found?

In almost all parts of the earth where there are large forests for them to range.

DOG.

What is this?

The dog.

For what is the dog useful?

He is a faithful servant to man; and, as he is permitted to accompany him, he feels proud; and, above all other animals, he is useful to defend his master's person and property.

Does the dog know more than most other animals?

He does; he loves and obeys his master, and always does as he is bid.

T. I hope my dear children will not suffer the dog to surpass them in obedience. Now you may repeat: —

I'll never hurt a little dog,
But stroke and pat his head;
I like to see the joy he shows,
I like to see him fed.
Poor little dogs are very good,
And very useful too,
For do you know that they will mind
What they are told to do?
And children all should surely be
As ready to obey:
Let us like them each token see,
And do as well as they.

BEAVER.

What kind of an animal is the beaver?

It is amphibious.

For what is the beaver remarkable?

For skill and industry.

In what does its conduct resemble man?

In forming societies do to a great work. Two or three hundred of them all work together in building their houses, and, when they have finished them, each family keeps to its own house.

Where do they build their houses?

By the water-side, as they are fond of bathing.

How do they build them?

They make them very nice; with three rooms, one above another.

Of what do they make their houses?

Of sticks of wood. They plaster them with clay, and keep them very clean. The houses are round, like an oven. Each beaver has a bed of moss to sleep on, and a store of food.

What is their food?

The bark of trees and small sticks, which they pile up very nicely.

Do they ever quarrel?

No; they live in peace, and appear quite happy.

Does it make children unhappy to quarrel?

It does; it is better to live in peace, and work as the beavers do.

Do men sometimes disturb their peace, and kill them?

They do, to get their skins, which have fur on them, which is useful in making hats; they also procure from beavers a medicine, called *castoreum*, which is found in bags of skin as large as an egg.

How large is the beaver?

It is as large as a common-sized dog, but very different in its form. Its teeth are remarkable for cutting. It will cut off large trees with its teeth, to make dams across the water.

Who has taught the beaver to do these things?

It is God, who made all creatures, and guides them by his wisdom.

THE CAMEL.

What ill-looking creature is this?

It is a camel.

Is it naughty, because it looks ugly?

O no, it is a very good animal.

What is it good for?

It will obey its master, and carry great loads of goods.

Of what other use is the camel?

It gives milk, which is good for food, and its hair is used to make clothing.

Where is this animal found?

In Asia and Africa.

How tall is the camel?

Six or seven feet.

Where is it most useful?

In the deserts of Arabia.

What is a desert?

It is a large country of sand, where no grass or trees grow, and no streams of water run.

Can camels travel in the desert without drinking water?

They drink enough at one time to last them several days.

How long does it take them to cross the desert?

Sometimes they travel several months before they get across.

What do they do for drink, then?

Their masters sometimes go out of their way to find water at a distance.

Can camels smell water before they see it?

They will smell water a mile off, and travel very fast, till they come to it.

Does one man go alone with his camel, and carry goods across the desert?

No; they are afraid to go alone, because of the robbers.

Who are these robbers?

Wicked men, in Arabia, who catch people in the desert and take away their goods.

How many men travel together in these deserts?

Sometimes one thousand men with their camels go together.

What is such a company of men and camels called?

A caravan.

How much can one camel carry?

A large camel will carry one thousand pounds.

How do men put so great a load upon their high backs?

The camel kneels down so low, when his master bids him, that it is easy to put on the load.

What will the camel do, if they put too heavy a load on him?

He will cry loudly, and will not rise till a part is taken off.

Do their masters drive them with a whip, as they do the horse?

No, they do not whip them; they sing or whistle to make them go; and the louder they sing the faster they will go.

Will they stop, when their masters stop singing?

They will. If their masters begin to sing to them they must continue singing till night, or they cannot make them go.

What did Joseph's brethren do, when they saw such a company of men and camels coming?

They drew Joseph up out of the pit, and sold him to them.

Other subjects in natural history may be used in the same way. An orange, grape, filbert, or some other vegetable, may be taken instead of a picture, and, when they can be obtained, will be preferable.

If any of the scholars have learned to read, they may be requested to repeat from memory all they can recollect about an animal, mineral, or vegetable, which has been described. Several books containing such accounts ought to be found in every school. Another exercise, to which you may direct the attention of the younger members of your school, is making letters, figures, etc., on a *blackboard* or slate. The former is an article of furniture indispensable in every school-room, and the latter should be furnished to every child, of whatever age. Variety, in the exercises of those who cannot read, is exceedingly important; and must be regarded, if you would make them happy.

Children may spell words by writing them on a slate nearly as early as they can spell orally; and, judging from experiments made, I know of few exercises either more useful or more pleasant to them.

LECTURE IX.

Young Ladies and Gentlemen: —

I offered some remarks in the last Lecture, with regard to the manner of teaching and interesting the younger members of your schools. The suggestions in this will have more particular reference to methods to be adopted in schools composed generally of older scholars. I shall attempt no more than to make some general suggestions, and express my own opinions. No one can follow out fully the plan of another. Each of you must make your own plan, after obtaining all the light you can on different modes. To aid you in forming such a plan, is all that I can hope to accomplish.

In the first place, I would have you guard against supposing that your whole duty consists in enabling your scholars to acquire a knowledge of the *books* put into their hands. This will be but a part, and sometimes a small part, of your duty. It is the subject, not the book, which is the more important. The book is the *instrument*, which you are to teach them how to use, in order to obtain the knowledge desired. To direct and assist them in this, and to lead them to exercise their own powers and elicit their own strength, is the principal duty of an instructor.

In teaching, let it be your first object to have everything *understood*. If the language in a text-book is unintelligible, or even some of the most important words are not understood, we obtain no *distinct* ideas. But let the thought be clothed in language with which we are familiar, and our attention is fixed, we are pleased and instructed; we obtain *ideas*, and may receive benefit.

Hardly anything is more common than for instructors to *presume* that their scholars understand subjects, when they do not. This error is increased by the decision of the pupil himself. "Do you understand this?" is often asked, and the learner answers, "Yes." The presumption that he does, too often satisfies the instructor, and the benefit the child might derive is lost. The teacher should interrogate the scholar till he ascertains whether he understands the subject; and if it should be found that he does, there will be an additional benefit to the pupil by an exercise of his powers in explaining it.

"I know, but cannot tell," is a reply that has

been given a thousand times, by children and youth, when I have asked a reason for rules and principles. "Why do you reject the 9's in proving the simple rules of arithmetic? and how do you know that this is a proper mode of proof?" "I know, but cannot tell." The scholar is *honest.* He supposes he *does* know, because he finds the directions in the rule are verified by the example in question. The learner misjudges. He believes he has the requisite knowledge, when he has not. If the teacher relies on the opinion of his pupil, he fails often of doing any service. The instructor should take measures to know whether the pupil understands a subject clearly. You should take nothing on trust; but question and examine till you *know* scholars understand the principles, and have correct views of the subject. When this is done you will have performed your duty, and not till then.

2. In your teaching, *use the most simple mode of illustration.* If an illustration be as little understood as the thing to be illustrated, the scholar remains as ignorant as before. When only one or two of the important words in the illustration are unintelligible, the scholar still remains ignorant. "Will you please to tell me why I carry one for every ten?" said little Laura to her instructor. "Yes, my dear," said he, kindly. "It is because numbers increase from right to left in a decimal ratio." Laura sat and repeated the words to herself two or three times, and then looked very sad. The teacher, as soon as he had

replied, pursued his other business, and did not notice her. But she was disappointed. She understood him no better than if he had used words of another language. "Decimal" and "ratio" were words that might have fallen on her ear before, but if so she understood them not. She looked in the dictionary, and was again disappointed, and after some time put away her arithmetic. When asked why she did so, she replied: "I don't like to study it; I can't understand it."

Now the injury to little Laura was very great. She had commenced the study with interest, and thus far had been pleased with it. She was now using a slate, and had found the direction, in adding numbers, to carry one for every ten. This she might have understood. The teacher loved his scholars, and wished to benefit them, but *forgot that terms perfectly plain to him might be unintelligible to a child.* From that moment, Laura disliked arithmetic; and every effort used with her, could not efface the impression that it was a hard study, and she could not understand it. Unimportant as this circumstance may appear to you, it made an impression on my own mind, which will not be effaced while I am engaged in teaching youth. The importance of the direction will be illustrated to you, doubtless, by a reference to your own history. You perhaps recollect many efforts made to explain a thing to you which have left you no wiser than before. Fail not, then, to use such language as can be understood by the child or by the class.

Be very careful to avoid the use of unintelligible words, by which they may become discouraged in their attempts to learn. It is of great importance, that the objects used to illustrate, should be those with the properties of which the pupil is acquainted. If you employ in the way of illustration any object, with the character of which the scholar is unacquainted, he is not in the least assisted. But if you can seize on something that he can see, or that he can recollect, or something with which he is familiar, and then make a just comparison, by which the idea is brought distinctly to his mind, he derives not only a lasting benefit, but present pleasure. For example: James came to his teacher, and told him he could not understand his map. He had just commenced the geography of his own State. The teacher called him to the desk, and took up a slate, and gave him a pencil, and then asked him if he could draw a plan of the school-room floor. James at once made his lines for the boundaries. "Now which is the east end?" James told. "Which is the west?" This he told also. "This is the north, and that is the south." "Now," said the instructor, "we will mark them, E for east," etc. "Now in what part is my desk?" "There," said the little fellow. "Where is the fireplace?" "There," said James. "Now, James, make marks for the boys' seats, and the girls' seats." He did this. "Now make marks for the doors and windows." This was done. "Now," said the teacher, "James, do you think you could make a map?" "No, sir," he replied. "Why yes you can; you have made one already," said the teacher. "This is a map of the floor. Now the map which you said you could not understand, is nothing more than this. There is a line for the east side, and there is another for the west side; and there is one for the north, and there is another for the south. Now these lines go round the whole State. This river is put down here, because it is in the northern part, and that river is represented there, because it is in the western. This river is drawn here, because it makes the eastern boundary of the State. Now look along here, and see if you can find the name of the town in which we live." "O yes," said James, "here it is." "Why is it put down here?" "Because it is in the east part of the State, near the river," said the child. The teacher asked him half a dozen similar questions, and James returned to his seat delighted. The simple illustration made everything easy. The other scholars were as much pleased as he, and when they were dismissed, were in high spirits, saying they would make a map of their gardens, orchards, etc., when they got home.

3. My next direction is, Let it be your object to make every study pleasant and interesting to pupils. This direction implies nothing impracticable or even difficult. The inquiry has been made, how is it possible to create a love of study in those who have no taste for it? "I feel little hesitation in asserting, that no such scholar ever existed,"

says Parkhurst, "unless he has been brought to feel this indifference or aversion by injudicious treatment on the part of parents or instructors. If parents or instructors love knowledge for its own sake, and always *speak* of study as a privilege and source of pleasure, children will be prepossessed in favor of it. When at school, if they receive lessons such as they can comprehend, if these lessons are explained to them in language they can understand, and if questions are asked which will bring other faculties of the mind as well as the memory into exercise, they will regard study pleasant. If teachers *expect* it to be pleasant to their scholars, they will endeavor to present subjects to them in such a light as to make it so."

This is always an object of importance, and "even in cases where parents counteract the impression which the teacher wishes to make, he may, by well-directed efforts, notwithstanding these discouragements, generally meet with a degree of success" sufficient to prove that children may be brought to love learning for its own sake, and be pleased with the acquisition of knowledge. "If the scholar is enabled to gain new ideas, or to form new combinations of those already gained," he cannot avoid being pleased. "Hence it is an object of primary importance" to teach them such things as "they can understand, either by their own reflections, or by the explanations and illustrations given them." What I recommend in this and in several previous directions, appears to have been achieved by *Pestalozzi.* Madame de Staël, in speaking of his school, says: "It is a remarkable circumstance, that neither punishment nor reward is necessary to excite his pupils in their labors. This is perhaps the first instance, where a school of one hundred and fifty children has succeeded without having recourse to the principles of emulation or fear. How many bad feelings are spared, when every emotion of jealousy and disappointed ambition is removed from the heart, and when the scholar sees not in his companions *rivals*, or in his teacher, a *judge!* Here the object is not to excel, not to succeed in a competition for superiority, but to make a progress, to advance towards an end, at which they all aim with equal integrity and sincerity of intention."

If *one* teacher has succeeded in making everything so pleasant that his scholars are interested and delighted with their studies, the same *may be* accomplished in other cases. Let it then be a daily study, with every instructor, so to present every study that it shall have attractions for the young. This may be done, generally, by employing the best modes of showing the importance of particular branches, the high value of knowledge, and by so calling into exercise the pupil's own powers, that he will neither be disheartened by difficulties, nor waste his energies in useless efforts. When a right course is taken with the young they are as happy at labor as at play,—as happy in school hours as during recess.

Among the subjects demanding particular attention in the school-room, spelling perhaps claims precedence. So soon as a scholar has learned the names of the letters, he must be occupied with their combinations. In our language, these combinations in the formation of words are often exceedingly irregular. The same letter has not only different sounds, but these different sounds are expressed by the use of very different letters.

Hon. Horace Mann, in a lecture before the American Institute, gives the following amusing illustration:—

"It is amusing to look back to the etymology of the words orthography and orthoëpy (which, in treating this subject, we have such frequent occasion to use), and to find that one of the Greek words from which each of them is derived, ὀρθὸς means *straight*, or *direct*. If *y-a-c-h-t* is a straight or direct way of spelling *yot;* or *p-h-t-h-i-s-i-c*, of spelling *tiz-ic*, I hope we may be delivered from knowing what *crooked* is. The five vowels, a, e, i, o, and u, ought to be called five harlequins. According to Worcester, these five letters alone have twenty-nine different sounds, namely, a, seven; e, five; i, five; o, six; and u, six. But the difficulty of their number is nothing, compared with that of their masquerading. In almost every line we read, these letters reappear several times; but, however short their exit from the stage, they reënter in a changed dress. Proteus is held a proverb of changeableness, but, compared with these, he was no turncoat, but a staid, uniform personage. To conceive of a child's difficulty, in giving their right sounds to the alphabetic characters, as found in words, let us suppose any five articles of furniture or dress, which we have most frequent occasion to use or to wear, were liable to change into twenty-nine articles of furniture or dress, the moment we should touch them; and, further, that this metamorphorsis were not only arbitrary but apparently wanton.

"But not only does the same letter puzzle us with its multiplicity of sounds, but different letters have the same sound; and combinations of letters assume the sound of individual letters; and they mock us by playing back and forth with the facility and the malignancy of evil sprites. Thus, as Mr. Pierpont has shown in his Little Learner, there are eight letters and combinations of letters which have the first sound of a, as in fate; namely, a, in date; ai, in paid; aigh, in straight; ay, in day; eh, in eh (exclamation); eigh, in eight; and ey, in they. So the first sound of e is given to e, in be; to ea, in bean; ee, in bee; ei, in seize; eo, in people; i, in machine; ie, in grief; and o, in you. The first sound of o is given to o, in note; oa, in boat; oe, in doe; oh, in oh (exclamation); ough, in borough; ow, in throw; owe, in owe; and eau, in beau. Again, ough appears in these different sounds; bough, cough, hough (the hinder part of the leg of a beast), though, thought, through, thorough, tough; and sure this is tough enough. It was on this combination, or rather dispersion, that the celebrated couplet was formed:—

'Though the tough cough and hiccough, plough me through,
O'er life's dark lough, I still my way pursue.'"

To acquire the habit of correct spelling, requires much time and very careful attention. However much we may desire to reduce these anomalies, we cannot. The labor of acquiring the orthography of our language must continue to be great. Exercises in spelling will necessarily occupy considerable time, and the best mode of conducting them demands the attention of every instructor.

It may be an inquiry, perhaps, when lexicographers, enjoying the best means for information, disagree, how learners are to know what is correct orthography? In reply, I remark, that the number of words with regard to which there is not uniformity is not very large. No one will be subjected to severe criticism who adopts and adheres to any respectable lexicographer, whether Webster, Johnson, Worcester, or Reid.

The great importance of this exercise should be a frequent subject of remark by every teacher, and the highest interest awakened in the minds of scholars. Let the example of teachers teach this. If they are careless or indifferent, such example will go far to prevent attention on the part of scholars.

The younger scholars should have an exercise in spelling as often as they read. Words may be selected from the reading lesson. Lessons from the spelling-book, for oral spelling or for writing should be short, and should not be passed over, till the learner can spell every word accurately. Lessons for spelling are usually *too long.* The learner is benefited more, by confining his attention to *ten* words for a lesson, and acquiring a thorough knowledge of these, than by being allowed to pass superficially over one ten times as long.

Another error extensively prevails. It is this. In order to make the word easier to be spelled, it is given with a pronunciation different from that used in reading or conversation. For example, the teacher pronounces the word *immediate.* The *i* in the third syllable has the sound of *e*. Instead of sounding it like *e*, he gives the *i* a distinct long sound, in order that the scholar may know it is not *e*; thus, im-me-d*i*-ate. Now this habit is very injurious to the scholar. The common sound will be on his mind, and he will be very liable to spell it wrong. Let this be a uniform rule: *Pronounce all words for a class to spell, just as you would pronounce them in reading or conversation.* That is, pronounce them right. And I would add, pronounce a word but *once*, and require the scholar to pronounce each syllable after spelling it. In some schools, the pupil is required to pronounce the word after the teacher, before attempting to spell it. This practice is no doubt beneficial. All who can write, should, at least once a day, write the words instead of spelling them orally. The teacher can devise any mode for ascertaining the errors, which he judges best. The scholars may exchange slates, or the slates may be brought to the teacher, if the class is small, or each scholar may examine the lesson and correct his own errors, and report his mistakes to the teacher.

The *method of teaching reading* is almost as various as the countenances of teachers. This branch requires more tact, and claims more attention, than any other. If the schools I have visited are a fair sample, I am obliged to say instructors are more generally deficient in their qualifications to teach reading successfully, than any other branch. Too long exercises are assigned, and scholars are allowed to read sentence after sentence, without being corrected, while they commit almost every kind of error conceivable. The first observations I shall make on this subject, will have reference to schools composed of *very young children*. Dunn* remarks: "The *Alphabet* is usually the first object presented to the notice of a child at school; and a more difficult or tiresome lesson he is never doomed to meet with in his whole future course. The *names* of the letters are unmeaning and arbitrary sounds; and with two or three exceptions, the *forms* are not associated with any object previously recognized. How can such an exercise be expected to produce anything but weariness and disgust? You will be glad to hear that men of the highest attainments in literature have not thought it beneath their character and standing to endeavor at least to facilitate the passage across this "bridge of sighs." Prof. Pillans proposes to arrange the alphabetic characters in brotherhoods, according to the organs of voice used in pronouncing them; and to teach the child the knowledge of his letters at first, and for a long time, in this way only. "We should thus avoid," he says, "the greatest difficulty the child encounters in learning the alphabet, that of recollecting the sequence or arrangement of the letters. The order of their succession in our common alphabet is entirely capricious, and appears, indeed, to be purely accidental; and a knowledge of it, so far from being indispensable at the outset, is at

* School Teacher's Manual.

that stage altogether useless for any practical purpose. Yet, in the ordinary way, the child is arrested, and unseasonably detained in the very porch of learning, by being compelled to name, and not to name only, but to learn by heart, a series of letters, which have not one associating tie to bind them in the memory, except juxtaposition. It is stringing beads, as it were, on a thread of sand. It may be well he should know this alphabetic arrangement when he comes to consult a dictionary; but I really cannot see its use for any other purpose. On the other hand, by the classification of letters in their cognate relations, the acquisition of them may be made an amusing exercise. The attention of the child being drawn to the organs of voice employed in each set, he makes experiments upon them, in imitating the sounds he hears, and has thus a guide to the pronunciation of each letter, which greatly facilitates his acquaintance with their form and power."

Jacotot, to whose principles and methods I may hereafter have occasion to refer, meets the difficulty in perhaps the best manner; he gets rid of alphabetic teaching altogether, and introduces the pupil, from the first, to a knowledge of words. At the Borough Road School, England, the *principle* of dispensing with alphabetic teaching has long been adopted: the alphabet class has merged in that of children in *two letters;* and all unmeaning combinations have been utterly excluded. The advantage is obvious. If the word " me," " in," or " to," for instance, be mentioned, the child recognizes a familiar sound, and, judging by the sound, he almost instinctively answers, m-e, to the question, " Can you spell the word me ?" If, after having mentioned the word, the teacher tells him to point on the lesson to the letters which compose it, his curiosity is excited, and the gratification attendant on a successful effort, excites a desire to encounter new difficulties.

Prof. Stone remarks : " Where no better course can be devised, the following is recommended, as it may be adopted in connection with any of the approved reading and elementary books now in use. The alphabet, name and form, may be taught analogically, in the usual way, by being impressed on the memory in repeated rehearsals, while pictures, infant school cards, and primers are used to awaken attention. As variety is always pleasing, children may sometimes march together, all saying the letters aloud, — sometimes sing an easy tune, perhaps " Auld Lang Syne," arranged to " a b c d, e f g h," — and sometimes read by themselves.

Monosyllabic sentences may be read, after the alphabet is learned ; and, if they can be selected in the form of interesting dialogue, they may with propriety engross considerable time.

At this early stage of education, natural defects, such as lisping, stammering, nasal enunciation, and inability to speak particular letters, as " *l*, *r*, *b*, *p*, *d*, *w*," require attention. Faults of this kind, which, in riper years, would baffle the most skilful management, may be easily removed by a little care at this age. The following suggestions have all been tested by experiment, and for want of room will be offered without theoretical explanation.

Let a lisper be instructed to hiss, or speak the *elementary sound* of " *s*," or soft " *c*," *with his tongue behind the upper teeth.* Lisping, and other faults, are often occasioned by a *web* or *string* under the tongue, which may be removed by the physician's lancet. Some sounds, as of " *b*, *d*," are more likely to produce stammering than others. These elements should be first ascertained, then carefully avoided, in all reading lessons. Easy flowing poetry, and sentences in which the open vowels occur most frequently, should be read with a full and loud voice, until the convulsive stoppage of the organs cease to appear. When a child is unable to speak " *w*, *p*," or any other letters, he should be directed to *imitate* by sight the position of the teacher's tongue, and other organs in making them.

Persons speaking with the *nasal twang*, are generally in the habit of breathing with the *mouth open.* Let the mouth be constantly closed, and as the breath must then pass through the nostrils, they will become sufficiently enlarged, in a short time, to afford free passage to sound.

Most of the difficulties experienced by children, in trying to make clear and articulate sounds, arise, not from defective organs, but from the fact that they do not know *how* to use them.

Children who are able to read monosyllables

with ease, but are still liable to hesitate upon *long* words, should read *very slowly*. The most disagreeable tones are formed and cultivated, by the rapidity with which children are often allowed to read. They should spell frequently, dividing the words into syllables, as this will be of great importance in enabling them to speak each element distinctly. As far as possible, their lessons in reading should be *colloquial*, and they should be permitted to criticize one another occasionally, and to imitate the teacher's voice, in repeating sentences. The use of stops should also be impressed upon their minds, and they be carefully trained to make their pauses naturally ; perhaps by counting aloud one at a comma, two at a semicolon, etc., until the pauses are familiar. They should understand, however, that pauses are subservient to *sense*, and that no exact time can be assigned to them.

To read with propriety and elegance is an interesting and valuable accomplishment. It should be the object of every instructor, to have scholars attend to all the principles exhibited by the best authors, and to read with a due degree of loudness, distinctness, and slowness ; and to regard the importance of accent, emphasis, and cadence. I shall give but few additional directions on this subject, but ask you to consult the suggestions made in the best reading books. The following must suffice : —

1. When a class is called out to read, devote your whole attention to it. It is a great error to

let them read as they please, and disregard the pauses and sense entirely. Let it be known as a regulation of the school, that, when a class is reading, no one has leave to ask a question or to change his place.

2. Require every scholar to pronounce every syllable so distinctly, that you can hear and understand the words. Many instructors fail here, from the fact that they hold a book, and have their eyes on the word that the scholar is pronouncing, and understand what it is from reading it, and not from *hearing* it read. Hence, it may be well to hear a class read at least once every day, without taking a book. It will then be easily learned how many syllables are not distinctly sounded by the young pupil. He should be required to read every sentence till he reads it right. In this way he will be made to improve more in reading a single page, than he otherwise would in reading half his book. It will be advantageous for the teacher to question the class, on the subjects of distinctness, slowness, emphasis, etc., before the lesson is commenced.

3. Be careful to show every scholar not only the importance and use of the stops or points in reading, but also of inflections, and require him to observe them. The pauses and inflections are of very great consequence. Without attention to them no one can be a good reader. If scholars form a habit of neglecting them, when young, it will be very hard to correct this habit afterwards. What is more disagreeable than monotony ? What

more unpleasant than to hear all the words of a sentence pronounced alike, or with so rapid an utterance that none are distinct? Much attention should be paid to these directions.

4. Be careful to lead your class to examine the character of the lesson to be read; and to make the manner and tone of voice correspond to it. To this direction, a degree of attention adequate to its importance is seldom paid in district schools. To read a pathetic piece in the same manner as you would one of Æsop's fables; or, to read a prayer in the same tone of voice that you would one of the humorous essays of Addison, is certainly unnatural and improper. And yet, in many of the schools which I have had occasion to visit, I have heard pieces of very different characters read in the same manner, and I have scarcely ever observed adequate attention paid to the subject. The fault lies with teachers. The directions given in books are disregarded, and the same monotony is permitted which was probably common in the schools they attended. I would not say that this remark is universally true; there are exceptions, but the remark will still hold true in relation to a great part of instructors. The style and manner of reading has not greatly improved for the last quarter of a century.

5. Let it be the object of every teacher, to côpy nature in his own reading, and then he will be sure to read with ease to himself and pleasure to his hearers. Scholars will readily copy the teacher's tones of voice and manner, and be led

to form a taste for this important acquisition. In reading on a mournful or playful subject, the manner and tone of voice will correspond to it, that the sense of the writer may be expressed. As far as possible, we should enter into the feelings of the writer, and utter his words very nearly as we suppose he would utter them, if he were reading his own language to us. I will only add: Strive to excel in this exercise, and to become as nearly perfect as possible; then you will hardly fail to awaken interest in your scholars, and greatly benefit them.

LECTURE X.

YOUNG LADIES AND GENTLEMEN: —

THE subject of arithmetic will next claim your attention. It is one which may be very early commenced. Indeed, as soon as the child has learned to count twenty, he may be taught to add, subtract, multiply, and divide. He may thus at a very early age form distinct ideas of the "ground rules of arithmetic," as before intimated.

With regard to the best mode of proceeding with a class in intellectual arithmetic, different teachers greatly differ in opinion. The method recommended by Mr. Colburn, is adequately explained in his treatise. But with a teacher* of long experience, I fully believe that no one who pursues his method would ever develop his powers of mind. "Those who, without much assistance, labor from day to day over a perplexing question, often acquire more mental strength, depth, and reach of thought, than those who, with the help of some appropriate and familiar illustration, think themselves, and are thought by others, perfectly to understand the whole. It is by the amount of thought, more than by an easy or ready comprehension of the subject, that the mind is strengthened, made quick and powerful." That mode of teaching is best, which leads the pupil most patiently to study a subject for himself, and to reason most accurately on the principles involved or the instruments to be used. I must believe that, while the analytic method is alone used, the child derives but a part of the benefit he ought.

I will, as concisely as possible, state the method I have pursued for many years; and which has succeeded best in my own schools. If you can form a better one for yourselves, adopt it; if not, the following may be of use. I refer to the text-book of Mr. Colburn, because that work is doubtless more common than any other, not because I think it is better or as valuable as some of the treatises recently prepared. The method will as well be employed with any other text-book.

When the learner has become familiar with the exercises in adding and subtracting in the first

* Rev. Mr. Perry, Lecture before American Institute, 1833.

section, and has become prepared to commence multiplication, I have required him, instead of giving the answer, merely to give the process of reasoning by which he obtains the answer, and knows that it is right, and to give the reason for that process. For example, the instructor inquires, What are two barrels of flour worth, at five dollars a barrel?

Pupil. Two times five dollars, which are ten dollars.

Inst. Why?

Pupil. Since one is worth five dollars, two, being twice one, must be worth two times as many; and two times five are ten.

Inst. What cost seven pounds of sugar, at eight cents a pound?

Pupil. As one pound costs eight cents, seven pounds will cost seven times eight cents, which are fifty-six cents.

Inst. How many farthings in ninepence?

Pupil. As there are four farthings in one penny, in ninepence there are four times nine farthings, which are thirty-six farthings.

Inst. If six men can do a job of work in eight days, how many men will be required to do it in one day?

Pupil. As six men do six days' work in one day, it will take eight times six men to do the job in one day, which is forty-eight men.

Inst. How many shillings are two reams of paper worth, at five dollars a ream?

Pupil. Two times five times six shillings, which are sixty shillings.

Inst. Why?

Pupil. Because each ream of paper is worth five dollars, and each dollar is worth six shillings; therefore, the paper is worth two times five times six shillings.

Exercises in division require a process the reverse of this, which will be as easily comprehended.

Quest. How many apples, at two cents apiece, can you buy for ten cents?

Ans. Since two cents will pay for one apple, ten cents will pay for one half of ten apples, which are five apples.

Quest. How many pears, at three cents apiece, can you buy for twelve cents?

Ans. One third part of twelve pears.

Quest. Why?

Ans. Because, as one pear costs three cents, you can buy a third part as many pears as you have cents.

Quest. How many pence in twelve farthings?

Ans. One fourth of twelve pence.

Quest. Why?

Ans. Because, as four farthings make a penny, there must be a fourth of twelve pence in twelve farthings.

After these exercises have been sufficiently pursued, both of these processes may be combined, as in the following examples: —

Quest. How many apples, at two cents apiece, can you buy for four lemons, at four cents apiece?

Ans. One half of four times four apples.

Quest. Why do you say one half of four times four *apples?*

Ans. The answer demanded is, apples; and the number of apples required must be half as large as the number of cents the lemons are worth. One lemon being worth four cents, four lemons are worth four times four cents; and as one apple costs two cents, you can buy one half of four times four apples, which are eight apples.

Quest. How much cloth, at five shillings a yard, can you buy for two reams of paper, at five dollars a ream?

Ans. One fifth part of two times five times six yards; that is, one fifth as many yards as the number of shillings the paper is worth.

Quest. How much wheat, at eight shillings per bushel, can you buy for two tons of hay, at eight dollars a ton?

Ans. One eighth part of two times eight times six bushels, which are twelve bushels.

Quest. Five men bought a horse for sixty-three dollars, and paid two dollars a week for keeping him eight weeks, and then sold him for fifty-four dollars; what did each man lose by the bargain?

Ans. Each man lost one fifth of sixty-three dollars, plus two times eight dollars, minus fifty-four dollars, which is five dollars.

[The terms *plus* and *minus* may be fully understood and applied by children six or seven years of age.]

Quest. Why?

Ans. Each man lost a fifth part of the sum all lost; and all lost what the horse and his keeping cost more than what they received for him when sold.

Quest. If eight yards of cloth cost thirty-two dollars, what will be the price of three yards ?

Ans. Three times one eighth of thirty-two dollars, which is equal to twelve dollars.

Quest. Why ?

Ans. Because three yards will cost three times as much as one yard ; and if thirty-two dollars is the price of eight yards, the price of one yard will be one eighth part of thirty-two dollars.

Quest. A man sold his watch for sixty-three dollars, which was seven ninths of what it cost him. How much did it cost him ?

Ans. Nine times one seventh part of sixty-three dollars, which is eighty-one.

Inst. How do you prove this ?

Pupil. Sixty-three dollars is seven ninths of the cost, and nine times a seventh part of sixty-three dollars must be the cost of the watch.

Quest. Two thirds of nine is three fourths of what number ?

Ans. Four times one third of two times one third of nine, equal to eight.

Quest. Why ?

Ans. Because two thirds of nine, which is six, is three fourths of the number sought. If six is three fourths, a third of six is one fourth of that number ; and four times one third of six, which is eight, is the number sought.

Quest. Six sevenths of fourteen is four ninths of what number ?

Ans. Of nine times one fourth of six times one seventh of fourteen, which is twenty-seven.

Quest. Seven ninths of eighteen is two fifths of what number?

Ans. Of five times one half of seven times one ninth of eighteen, which is thirty-five.

Inst. Prove that seven ninths of eighteen is two fifths of thirty-five.

Pupil. One fifth of thirty-five being seven, two fifths is fourteen, and fourteen is seven ninths of eighteen.

Quest. Three sevenths of twenty-eight, is two eighths of how many times seven?

Ans. Of one seventh of seven times one sixth of four times one fifth of thirty, equal to six and six sevenths.

Quest. Four sevenths of sixty-three is six eighths of how many ninths of forty-five?

Ans. One fifth of eight times one sixth of four times one seventh of sixty-three, equal to nine and three fifths.

By a course of this kind, you may accustom the scholar to examine carefully the question, or proposition, and lead him always to inquire,—

1. What is required to answer the question proposed?

2. What means are furnished by the conditions of the question for obtaining the required answer?

It is very important to keep constantly before the mind of a learner, that if one half, or one third, or one tenth, etc. of any number is stated, the entire number is distinctly implied; also, if six sevenths, nine tenths, twelve twentieths, etc. of any number is given, both one seventh, one tenth, one twentieth, is indirectly given; and if so, the entire or whole number is implied.

By the foregoing questions and answers, it is intended to give nothing more than a bare exposition of the method proposed. Any intelligent teacher will readily perceive the design from a few examples only. Children, not more than seven or eight years of age, of ordinary capacity, have been found fully able to solve any questions in Colburn's manual, by the above method. The subsequent progress of such in written arithmetic, has always been rapid, compared with others of similar age and capacity, who have not been taught by the method described in the foregoing remarks.

In teaching written arithmetic successfully, several things must be aimed at by the instructor.

Let it be a first object to lead the learner to investigate the reasons on which rules are founded. This is a direction of great importance. If he forms the early habit of inquiring why the direction is given for each step in his operation, he will be likely to proceed understandingly from the beginning. But if he is directed to go to his rule, or commit it to memory, and then apply it to the performance of his operation, he will probably be led to suppose that when he has obtained a correct answer, he understands the subject. He may go *through* with a common treatise on arithmetic in this way, and yet not understand the reasons on which the directions, even in the "ground rules," are founded. "I have ciphered through," is often said by a young person, who, in fact, would find it very difficult to explain the reasons of the rule given for multiplication or division.

With all the attention such pay to arithmetic, they are but poorly prepared for the common business transactions of life. Many persons formerly were aware of this, and therefore provided themselves with a "ciphering-book," and wrote down the operations in it for future use. In this way, much more time was spent than would have been necessary to obtain a knowledge of arithmetic adequate to the wants of life, in such a way that the knowledge would be permanently retained.

When any engage in this study, whether they are beginners or not, it is proper for you to begin with the simple rules, and question them on all the principles which have led to their formation. If the pupil can give you proper answers, it is well; if not, let him continue his attention to first principles till he can. Afford him assistance, if he cannot find out the principle for himself. If possible, let that assistance be given in such a way as shall make him his own teacher. What I mean is, ask him questions which will lead him to the right track, and will cause him necessarily to arrive at a satisfactory conclusion. I may be better understood, perhaps, by an example. A class is called to recite the rule of multiplication.

The teacher inquires, What is multiplication?

Class. Multiplication teaches, having two numbers given to find a third, which shall contain either of the given numbers as often as the other contains a unit.

Inst. Well, so your book says; but what does it mean? Can either of you explain it so that John, who has just commenced the rule, can understand it?

Class. [After hesitating some time.] No, sir; we cannot.

Inst. Think: cannot you use some other language, which will make it more intelligible?

Class. May it not be called a short way of adding?

Inst. Yes; and that explains it much better than the long definition which you recited. Can you tell me now, why it may be called short addition?

Class. Because it is the same as adding one of the numbers to itself as many times as there are units in the other. If we wish to multiply 3 by 5, it will be the same as writing 3 five times, or 5 three times, and adding them together.

Inst. Very well; now tell me why two numbers are given, and not any more, to perform the operation?

Class. If there be more than one multiplicand, there must be more than one answer, and if there be more than one multiplier, the multipliers will be component parts of each other, and therefore would in reality be but one.

Inst. Why do you place one under the other?

Class. To make the operation more convenient. The work might be done if the numbers were differently placed.

The instructor may proceed to ask the following questions: Why do you begin at the right hand to multiply? Why do you multiply the whole multiplicand with the right-hand figure of the multiplier, before you multiply with the others? When you begin to multiply with the second figure, why do you put the product one place to the left of the first figure of the line above it. What is the value of the first product figure, in the second line? is it units or tens? When you have taken the third figure of the multiplier, why do you set the first figure of the product still farther to the left, and under the figure by which you multiply? What is the value of the first figure in the third line of the product; is it units, tens, or hundreds? Why do you add all the lines of the product in order to obtain your answer? How do you prove the result? How do you cast out the nines? Why will this prove it? Will it prove it to cast out the 7s or 8s? Why not? Why do you take 9 rather than another number? Is there any other number that will prove it? Why will 3 or 18 answer as well as 9? If the multiplier be 9, how can the work be shortened? Why will the placing as many ciphers at the right of the multiplicand as you have 9s in the multiplier, and then subtracting the multiplicand once out, give the same answer as to multiply by the 9s contained in the multiplier?

Answers to such questions, and many others, will be necessary in order to make the rule intelligible. But the scholar will not perhaps think of them, unless interrogated by the teacher. If any of these answers cannot be given by your scholars, after opportunity is afforded them to reflect, let your own explanation be as simple as possible. It is a useful exercise for a pupil to form a set of questions to each rule for himself, before being examined upon it. After he has thus formed all the questions he is able, you may make such additions as you think requisite. In this way he will be led to reflect on the given rule, and will strive to understand the principles on which it is founded. He will not only gain more knowledge, but he will gain it in a way that will enable him to retain it longer, and apply it more readily, than by the common method.

Make the *principles* on which every rule is founded thoroughly *understood;* let a portion of the time spent in the *mere practical* part be devoted to acquiring a thorough acquaintance with the *reasons* on which rules are founded, and we have every reason to apprehend these *principles* will remain in the memory when the details shall be forgotten.

Encourage the learner to continual effort, rather than to work out a difficult problem for him. When he accomplishes it himself, he will not soon forget the manner, and is encouraged to employ his own powers, instead of leaning on his instructor.

Geography will undoubtedly claim considerable attention in your schools. To teach it in the best way is desirable. The question, what is the best mode? would be answered very differently by different individuals.

The mode generally pursued is, to present a child with a map of the world; to teach him its general divisions, and how to distinguish them on the map, bound them, etc. This mode has been approved by most instructors; but I am willing to confess, it has appeared to me the very opposite of the course that reason would dictate. Why should we attempt to teach a child what he cannot comprehend? Why should he learn the names of continents, islands, oceans, seas, and lakes, rivers and mountains, many thousands of miles distant, before he is taught the geography of his own town, county, State, and country?

Where it is practicable, let the child be taught something of the geography of his own neighborhood, and especially of his own State, before he commences the study of it in a more extended manner. Let him be taught the boundaries of his own town; the names and situation of its mountains, rivers, ponds, and other interesting particulars. Then the same things may be taught him of the adjoining towns, the county, and the State. By this mode, he will be led to form some ideas of distance, and the size of places. He will be prepared to learn the same things in regard to other States, and his country and continent. From his own, he may pass to other countries and continents, until the features of the world are in succession brought distinctly to his view.

Endeavor to have the outlines, the more general facts, *very thoroughly acquired.* These should always be distinguished from the subjects in detail. They will be a guide to other knowledge, and will, without doubt, be better remembered than if associated with a multiplicity of facts in detail.

Prominent facts in geography should be learned in such a way as to be easily remembered. This is secured only on the principle of classification. Rivers of equal length, mountains of the same height, and cities of the same population, may be arranged in classes, according to the principle of Woodbridge, with great advantage. Most persons remember facts associated with other facts more readily than in any other way. Much time is lost by attempting to crowd the memory with too many unimportant facts. A few things learned very thoroughly will be worth much more than a vastly greater number of things learned superficially. Let the boundaries of our own country, and of the individual States, be very thoroughly fixed in the memory, and the leading things of interest with regard to other parts of the world, and the learner derives more benefit than by attempting so much that he remembers nothing perfectly. Let the pupil " begin the study of each country, with the consideration of its physical condition and resources, as developed in his previous views of the world. He should observe the extent of its sea-coast, the number and size of its streams, the general character of its climate, as affected by its place upon the globe, and by peculiar circumstances, and the vegetable productions to which it

17

is adapted. He should then be taught any peculiarities which exist in its physical character, and should be led to infer from the whole its capacities and resources, and the employments most likely to promote the welfare of its inhabitants.

" A closer view of its political, social, and religious institutions, and habits, will too often present sad obstacles to the accomplishment of the best plans, and he should next be taught the actual condition of knowledge, of morals and agriculture, and arts and commerce, as resulting from the combined action of physical and moral causes. He should be led to appreciate the national character connected with these circumstances, so far as this can be done with accuracy, and without that gross injustice which sometimes attributes the peculiarities of a small class to the people of a whole country; which would make the Portuguese all assassins, and the people of New England a nation of peddlers. He should study also the topography of the country, its principal towns and cities, and its most important public institutions, humane, religious, and literary.

" This survey should be completed by an examination of its statistics, the number of its inhabitants, the manner in which they are distributed, the density of population, the amount of commerce, manufactures, revenue, and public debt, and the magnitude of its army and navy. The extent to which these details should be carried must of course be varied according to the character and circumstances of a pupil, and the time which may be devoted to this study. They should be carried so far as the judgment of the pupil can employ them, in estimating the state and resources of the country. They should never be so extended as to burden the memory. These, however, cannot be retained with facility, nor can they be employed for the purpose of comparison, for which numbers are chiefly useful, without some species of classification.

"On such points, particularly, all our conceptions of great and small, many and few, are founded entirely upon comparison. It is far more important and useful to the pupil, to know that London contains as many people as the whole State of Virginia, than to be able to tell the precise number of inhabitants in either; and the population of both would be more easily remembered by associating them together. And his conception of the populousness of a town or city, which approaches his own in magnitude, will be much more associated by telling him that it is twice, or thrice, or ten times as large as his native place, than by stating the precise number of people it contains. Few persons can estimate or conceive of numbers of people, even to a few hundreds or thousands, much less of an equal number of square miles. The mind is confused by higher numbers, and can only arrive at distinct conceptions by referring to some known standard, approaching in magnitude to that presented, instead of being obliged to compare it with unity." *

* Woodbridge.

It is also important to exhibit the facilities of obtaining the necessaries and conveniences of life, furnished by different climates and countries; also the inconveniences and privations peculiar to any section of the world, on which the lesson of the class may be. This is recommended for the purpose of comparison with our own happy land, and for showing the general providence of God, who has so constituted things that one part of the world is dependent on another for some of the conveniences of life; also, for exhibiting the fact that no part of the world is unprovided with the means of promoting human happiness, and no portion is exempt from evils of some kind. The most productive regions of the earth are often visited with dreadful storms and tempests. Troublesome insects, poisonous serpents, and the most ferocious beasts, annoy the inhabitants of some parts, where otherwise a residence might almost be compared to one in paradise. Scholars will always be interested by remarks on subjects of this kind; and not only so, they will derive lasting benefit from them.

Accustom your scholars to draw maps on slates from recollection. If they know this will be required of them, they will examine the situation of places, mountains, rivers, etc., with much more attention than otherwise, and will probably retain the knowledge which they acquire much better than if not required to attend to this exercise. The instructor, at the close of the recitation, should examine the slates, and point out the deficiencies or errors. Outline maps may be used with great advantage by the skilful instructor, when a class has made considerable proficiency in the study.

In directing the studies of a class in geography, it should be kept in mind that a few leading and important facts are of greater value than a multitude of unimportant particulars; that much time is lost by attempting to acquire so much that but little is accurately committed to memory, and retained.

English grammar is included in the list of studies to be pursued at common schools. All who offer themselves as teachers in these schools are examined in this branch. It is the duty of all such to qualify themselves, to give thorough instruction in it. But I am constrained to believe that instructors are, to a great degree, deficient in this respect. I do not intend to affirm, that there is not considerable familiarity with the rules of syntax, as these rules are stated by some one author. It has long been a question, whether the present mode of pursuing this study, or of teaching it, does not require greater modification than any other. To say that the mode of teaching grammar most usual in district schools should be improved, is saying merely what is proved by the fact that it is usually considered dry and uninteresting by a great majority who attend to it; and of course very little advancement is made in it. The more usual method is to put a book into the hands of the scholar, and require him to commit certain parts of it to memory; and, when this is done, he is called upon to parse sentences and apply the rules of syntax. Parsing is continued year after year, without much attention to anything but deciding on the parts of speech and applying rules. When he is able to tell the part of speech at sight, and refer to rules applicable to the several words in a sentence, he is often called a good grammarian, and not unfrequently considered qualified to be an instructor of others. But after all, it may be doubted whether he is better acquainted with grammar than some have been who have never studied the rules of syntax. That this mode occupies much time to little profit, I think must be conceded by all. While I make this remark, I wish not to be considered as a convert to the doctrine of those masters, who have professed the ability to teach grammar in a month, or even half of that time. The call for reform in teaching this branch is loud. Much time is spent to very little purpose, both in common schools and academies.

If a better mode of teaching than the following can be adopted, I would advise you to pursue it. If you are inclined to judge favorably of the following directions, it will probably be found by you that the system contains one advantage, at least; that of making the study pleasing. Among a very large number with whom I have pursued it, I have seldom found any who complained that grammar was unpleasant or dry.

1. Let it be an object to explain to your scholars what grammar is, and the importance of un-

derstanding the nature of their own language. This must lead them to see that, in attending to this study, they are not learning that which is useless or unnecessary. They will be made acquainted with its usefulness by familiar illustration; and when this is accomplished, they will commence the study with far more interest than otherwise. The exact meaning of the four subjects on which it treats, should be fully explained. The child often has not the most distant idea, that, while he is learning to spell words, he is learning grammar. Etymology is often unintelligible; but show him how words are derived from each other, and how the part of speech is affected by varying the word, and he will become interested.

To illustrate. Take the word *man*, and show him how many words come from it; or require him to tell all the words which he can recollect, and then explain the meaning which each has, and why they are classed with different parts of speech; as *man*, a noun; *to man*, a verb; *manning*, a participle; *manful*, an adjective; *manfully*, an adverb; and *manliness*, another noun. With an exercise of this kind he will be pleased, and will be obtaining the meaning of many words which he would not otherwise learn.

Time is usefully employed in attending to the composition of compound words, and the meaning of such, ascertained from the meaning of the root, and the parts connected with it. For instance, "take the word *retrospection;* the teacher would direct, 'Separate it,' and the learner would reply, '*retro*, behind; *spect*, look; and *tion*, act or action.' The teacher would then say, 'What is the meaning of the word *retrospection?*' and would ask for other instances in which the root occurs. In-spect, pro-spect, spect-acle, circum-spect, re-spect, and other words would be given."

"The advantages of this course are numerous and weighty. It teaches the scholar to study the character of every word, as it is brought before him. It leads the mind also from the words to observe the legitimate use of them, the communication of ideas. By inducing the learner to draw on the resources of his own mind, it teaches him to compare, to discriminate, to judge; a process by which he is rendered capable of far greater mental exertion. It necessarily insures a habit of observation and scrutinizing inquiry; it occasions close application; and it constantly calls upon the teacher rather to restrain than to excite."

2. When it becomes proper to have a scholar begin the grammar, or text-book, let him first learn the definition of the most common parts of speech; as, the noun, pronoun, and verb. Then let him take a sentence and select all the nouns in it, and tell why they are nouns; all the pronouns, and tell why they are pronouns; and all the verbs, and tell why they are verbs. The next lesson may be to learn the different kinds of nouns and articles, and what belongs to each; and then he should select the nouns in a sentence, and tell why they are nouns; what kind, and why; what number, and why; what gender, and why; what person,

and why. Also the articles, and tell why they are articles; what kind, and why they are of that kind. Let the scholar proceed in this way through the pronoun and verb, and then learn the definitions of other parts of speech. He should then be taught to parse all the words of a sentence in course, and tell what each word is, define it, and give his reason for everything he says about it. In this way, he will learn understandingly, and will be able to see why these definitions and rules have been given, which he is now called upon to commit to memory.

After he can demonstrate easily, he may be directed to commit to memory some of the most important rules of syntax, and apply them to the language which he passes. He should be asked, when he says, "the nominative case governs the verb," or "a verb agrees with its nominative case," how the rule applies to the case in question, and on what principle it is founded? And though he may not always be able to give an answer, yet, by having been asked the question, he will be more likely to recollect the explanation which you may give, and be able to repeat it when you ask him again. A mode like the above, pursued through the whole of grammar, will leave nothing dark to the mind of the scholar.

3. When the rules of syntax are acquired, and he can apply them with facility, he will be prepared to analyze sentences, and should be taught to distinguish between a sentence and phrase, a simple and compound sentence, and also to know

what are the principal parts of a sentence; as the subject, attribute or predicate, and object.

The exercise of showing how words are derived one from another should be continued, and the pupil be accustomed to point out the different parts of speech which may come from a single word. He will, by this, be able to see the dependence of one word upon another, and learn to discriminate the character of each.

In this connection, I would recommend giving him sentences in which there is some grammatical error for him to detect, and to give his reason for thinking it an error. This exercise is very important, as it will lead him to guard against errors in the formation of sentences, and will help him to apply the knowledge which he has acquired to practical purposes. In selecting sentences for this purpose, it will be well to take them from the conversation of the scholar himself, or such language in common use as is ungrammatical. This will lead him to examine his own language by the rules which he has learned, and enable him to detect his own errors.

In this as in other studies, the important laws of the language, the most important definitions and most essential rules, should be very *thoroughly* acquired. In this way only, the learner is able to recall and apply rules to his own language, or the language of others.

It will be expected that you should instruct your scholars in penmanship. This is a very necessary accomplishment; but it would be better, if it could be taught in a school where it should be the only branch. Yet long custom has placed it among the requisitions of a common school. It is not possible, I think, at present, to obviate this inconvenience; and the only inquiry is, how we may make it the least injurious to other branches of study, and secure the greatest improvement therein. The result of my own experience has been, that three quarters of an hour, devoted once a day exclusively to this exercise, is better than a longer period, and is the least likely to interfere with other studies. The following are all the directions for which I have time.

1. Prepare all the books for writing at your own room, and furnish the copies which will be necessary for the day. If the books are not ruled for writing, I would recommend to you to do it yourselves, when you prepare the copies. This will save much time to the school, and prevent much disturbance from the noise of borrowing rules, or frequent removals to get and use them. The copies ought to be prepared before you come into school, in order to have your whole time when there to devote to other objects. When the hour appointed for writing arrives, let everything else be dropped by those who are to write; let them take their books and pens, and attend only to their writing.

2. While the scholars are writing, devote your whole attention to them. See that every one sits in an easy and proper posture. Attend to the manner in which every pen is held, and see that

all write slowly. The instructor should go from scholar to scholar, and give such directions as are necessary. If the house is properly constructed, you will be able to go to every scholar in the class once in two or three, or at most, in five minutes, and will be able to direct in regard to the writing of every line, to point out errors and defects to be avoided. The progress of the pupil will depend very much upon the interest he is made to feel in the subject. Without attention, no progress of importance can be made.

3. When the time for writing has expired, let all the pens be cleaned at once, and the books returned. If scholars are permitted to continue writing, after the attention of the instructor is turned to other exercises of the school, they will often write carelessly, and make no improvement. When *one* ceases *all* should cease, and direct their attention to other things.

By pursuing a course like the above, there will be very little loss of time, and very little danger of the formation of careless habits. But if scholars are permitted to call for copies when they please, and to write as much and as carelessly as they please, they will greatly disturb the course of the school, and probably contract habits which will not be broken up without difficulty; they will waste paper and time, and make very little progress either in writing or in other studies.

4. In preparing copies, it is important to have a system. The easiest parts of letters should be first made, and a regular course of lessons given.

Unless some system is adopted, it will be impossible for the teacher to be uniform with himself. He will be liable to neglect some letters, while others are very frequently used in the copies. Every one who pretends to teach without following some system, will fail of teaching well.

History is a study which ought to be pursued in all our schools, at least so far as relates to the history of our own country. Every teacher should speak of it as a necessary study, and as one which will be very pleasant. Though there is no text-book which seems to me exactly adapted to common schools, yet there are many that contain valuable information; and by selecting subjects from them of the most interest, and making these plain to the understanding of the scholar, by such illustration as the nature of them will admit, children will be highly interested.

I would advise you to commence with a class, by giving very familiar lectures on the history of their own town or State, or the places with which they are acquainted. Then lessons from books, in regard to particular events which have taken place. Topics should be selected which relate to events connected, in an eminent degree, with the welfare of the country. When subjects are given them, instead of requiring them to take all the events in their connection, the class will be more likely to engage with interest in the exercises, and to retain what they learn. If these lessons are given, following the order of time in which the incidents occurred, a connected history of the prominent events will be obtained, and each general subject will be more firmly fixed in the mind.

To illustrate more fully what I mean. After a few general subjects, such as may relate to the history of the town, neighborhood, or State, I would recommend that the lessons be given out in a manner somewhat like the following: You may take your histories and learn, so that you can relate to me, the most important particulars relative to the first discovery of the country. I shall ask you these questions: Who discovered America? From what country was he? How many ships had he? What happened on the voyage? After his men had become disaffected, how long did Columbus persuade them to sail? What happened during that time? What did Columbus do when he arrived at the shore? What name did he give to the place? Whom did he find there? What was it that excited very much the attention of his men? What did the natives think of Columbus and his crew? What happened when they were on their homeward passage? How were they received? etc.

The next subject may be the first settlement of Jamestown; then, that of New England. The next, the history of the settlement of New York, and of its being taken by the English. "Now," you may say to them, "I wish you to take for your next lesson, the contest between the Colonies and England, and what was the consequence." Afterwards, the particulars of the battle of Lexington; then, that of Bunker Hill, etc. By proceeding in this way, and directing the pupil to fix his mind on but one subject for each lesson, he will be able to understand his lesson fully, and will read attentively everything that regards the subject on which he is to be examined.

I am confident that two objects will be secured by this mode, which are not gained as well by putting a book into the hands of a scholar and requiring him to learn the whole; namely, he will be better pleased, and will gain a more distinct knowledge of the most interesting facts. I would not say positively that the mode I have recommended is the best; but it has succeeded better than any I have known adopted in our schools. If the members of a class have different books, it will not be very material, as each author treats of all the most interesting facts in history.

Another subject ought to receive attention in all our schools, I am happy to know that it is introduced into many.

I refer to exercises in writing composition. "That which gives to any branch of study its value, is its practical utility." If this sentiment be just, composition should never be neglected. Every one who can write, has occasion to compose letters on business or friendship, and, in some way or other, to express his thoughts on paper more or less frequently. To neglect, while acquiring an education for common business, some things which are as important as others which receive *particular* attention, is not the dictate of reason. But this consideration is not the only evidence that this subject claims attention. Arranging our ideas in sentences, and combining those sentences so as to express a continued train of thought, is one of the best means of making the knowledge which we gain practical. Perhaps hardly any exercise is a better discipline of the mind than the writing of composition. It is the application of knowledge to the business of life. Without such application much that is acquired will be soon lost, and, if not lost, of what value can it be to its possessor? Of what use to the farmer were all the theory that might be obtained, if he never applied his knowledge to his business?

When composition is neglected in district schools, it becomes a very burdensome exercise to such as may afterwards attend a higher school or an academy. Many have I seen weep, when this was then made a requisition for the first time. "I was never called upon to write before, and now it seems to me that I cannot," has been said by many. "I wish I had been required to write when I attended the district school, and then it would not be such a task now."

The following directions may be of service to you on this subject.

1. Labor to impress the minds of the school with a sense of the great importance of this exercise. This may be done by representing the many situations in which they would highly value the art of expressing their thoughts on paper; the interest they will feel in being able to compose a letter to a friend in a handsome style; the

inconvenience they must often suffer, if they neglect this exercise till they are obliged to write and expose their ignorance, or make application to others to do that for them which they ought to be able to do for themselves. All this may be impressed upon their minds by means of familiar illustration.

2. It has been found profitable to commence with young scholars, by giving them a number of words, and requiring them to write a sentence, in which one or more should be used. The first words may be nouns, the next adjectives, the next pronouns, etc. Give the child a slip of paper, with the direction and words; as, for instance, the following: Write sentences, and use one of the following words in each: man, gold, stars, lines, eagerness, play, home, garden. Compositions should afterwards embrace a variety of other single words, or of words compounded. The object of this course is to make the task easy, to have the invention of the scholar brought into vigorous exercise, and to have him excited to learn the exact meaning of words. It is conceived that by such a mode all these objects are gained.

3. When the scholars are sufficiently exercised in this kind of composition, it may be useful to read a story, and then let them relate as much of it as they can remember, in their own words. This enables them to see the importance of paying close attention to what they hear, and of fixing the most prominent ideas, so as to treasure them up. But as they will not be likely to retain any full sentence, it leads them to the exercise of

arranging ideas in sentences, nearly as much as writing an original composition. They will not be discouraged on account of not knowing what to write, and will probably be amused and pleased with the exercise.

4. General subjects may be afterwards given, on which to write; subjects with which they *are* familiar, or *may become so* by reading. It is always better to *give* subjects, than to let the pupil *select* for himself; for he will often choose without judgment; or be frequently unable to decide on any subject; or he will often select the hardest subjects, thinking them the easiest. Of this kind are such as the following; friendship, love, hope, spring, summer, autumn, winter, youth, life, health, pleasure, hope, etc.

In selecting subjects, it is very important they should be such as will benefit the scholars in a moral point of view, or in supplying rules and precepts for the transactions of life. If a young person can be excited to a proper course of reflection on the influence which different habits will have upon his happiness and usefulness, he will be much more likely to cultivate those which are correct than he would do without such reflections. It is therefore of very great importance to lead the young to such considerations as shall be of the greatest benefit in the cultivation of correct habits. Such questions as the following, when given as subjects of composition, have been found very useful. What four things ought the young to seek first, in order to promote their own happiness?

What six habits may I form while young, that will secure to me the greatest personal enjoyment and respectability? By the formation of what five habits can I do the most good to my fellow-men? By what five habits can I most injure society? Describe the character of such persons or families as you would wish for your neighbors. Must the drunkard be an unhappy man? if so, why? Do you believe the thief, liar, etc., can be happy? if not, why? Why does God forbid theft, lying, etc.?

Questions on subjects of this kind may be multiplied and varied according to the judgment of the teacher, and may be rendered easier or harder, according to the ability of the class. The scholars thus not only derive satisfaction from the easy accomplishment of their tasks, but are excited to reflect, and to make up their opinions on subjects very important to them, while forming characters for life.

5. Recommend to your pupils to correspond with each other, to ask each other questions to be answered in writing, also to write down their own reflections for their own private use. The effect of this course will unquestionably be salutary. They will not only be excited to a cultivation of the social affections, but will undoubtedly be much advanced in tho art of composition. This knowledge, however, will not long be retained without practice. The necessity of this should be constantly urged. Everything which has a tendency to call forth their own powers of mind is important, and will be productive of good.

On another subject, it is highly important that you should communicate instruction. Moral philosophy may not perhaps, in a majority of schools, be introduced as a regular study, but you may make your scholars acquainted with some of its important principles, and teach them to examine the reasons of moral distinctions. You may direct them to examine the character of the things they approve, and of those they disapprove; why some things please and others displease them. They may be taught that in *all* persons there is implanted a moral sentiment, and this has a material influence on human happiness. You may inform them what feelings and what actions are virtuous, and what are vicious, by referring them to the great rule of duty, as presented in the law of God. Let no day pass without reading, or causing to be read, some portion of the sacred Scriptures. Appeal to this, as the standard by which all actions and habits are to be tried. Call the attention of your pupils to this remarkable fact: That whatever men generally agree conduces to unhappiness or misery, is forbidden or condemned in the Bible; and everything in which true enjoyment is found, is there approbated and commended or required.

LECTURE XI.

Young Ladies and Gentlemen: —

In the present Lecture, I wish to call your attention to several things which, though intimately connected with some previous topics, may perhaps be better presented in a separate Lecture.

The first is, the great importance of seizing on favorable opportunities to fix lasting impressions on the minds of your pupils. There will frequently occur seasons, when impressions may be made on the minds of the young much more readily than at others. The attention is awake, the mind becomes aroused, and impressions then made will be more lasting than when the mind is not excited. Such seasons should be regarded as a seed-time, which, if improved by the teacher, may be the means of producing very important fruits.

I shall be best understood by an example. An eclipse occurred during the hours of school. The darkness occasioned a suspension of labor for a season. After permitting the scholars to go and look at it, and at the objects around shrouded in gloom, the teacher returned with them to the school-room, and addressed them in the following manner: —

"You have seen," said he, "a most interesting sight to-day, and one which may lead you to some profitable reflections. The moon is a planet very small when compared with the earth or sun, and yet, by being near us, and coming between us and the sun, has obscured that light which is so cheerful and necessary. I wish to turn your thoughts for a moment to the interesting nature of the study of astronomy, by which the motions of the heavenly bodies may be perfectly known, and their size and distance determined with accuracy. I wish you to know also the importance of this science to us. If astronomers had not been able to tell us of this eclipse, and had we not expected it to-day, how great must have been our terror! We might have been as much frightened as some of the ancients are said to have been at similar appearances. But now we look upon it with the utmost delight, as a rare exhibition of the effect of planetary motion. Had you seen an astronomer calculating this eclipse five years ago, you might have said he was not doing anything to benefit you; but you now see how much terror and fear he has saved you, by telling you beforehand of the sublime spectacle of to-day. All the art which *he* had, is what *you* may easily acquire, by attending to the study of astronomy. Who is there that would not delight in a study so sublime and important? He who first learned that this eclipse would happen to-day, was once a little child, and knew no more than the most ignorant of you. You may, like him, become learned and wise. By resolutely and faithfully pursuing your studies, you may be able to understand all that others know of astronomy, or any other of the sciences which man has acquired. But he among you who is unwilling to persevere in obtaining knowledge, must continue to be ignorant of that which others know. Now who of you will choose to be ignorant, and who of you will endeavor to be wise? I shall know your individual determinations, by observing who of you are hereafter faithful in improving your time, and who among you choose play and ignorance, in preference to application and wisdom."

Take another example; one of actual occurrence. It was a chilly day of winter, and we were all seated in a comfortable school-room. A man of most wretched appearance was seen passing by, drawing a hand-sled, on which were several bundles of woollen rags, the remnants of garments worn till they could be of no further use. He was clad in those but little better, and was apparently so weak as to be scarcely able to draw his sled. Some looked out of the window and began to laugh. The instructor saw him, and remarked: "You may all rise up and see that wretched man, passing by." They did so, and nearly all were diverted to laughter. After all had seen him, the teacher told them they might take their seats, and then remarked: "I was willing you should look at that man, but possibly my object was very different from yours, as I see the effect on your feelings was very different from what was produced on mine. That miserable man, you at once perceive, is crazy. He has bundles of rags on his sled, which perhaps he values, though they can be of no service to him. You perceived he looked pale and emaciated; he was so weak as scarcely to be able to draw his load. He is very poorly shielded from the cold of winter, and will very probably perish in the snow. Now tell me, my scholars, does this man excite your laughter? He was once a school-boy, sprightly and active as any of you; his return from school was welcomed by joyful parents, and his presence gave pleasure to the youthful throng, who met each other in a winter evening for merriment and sport. Look at him now; and can you sport with him who has lost his reason, and, in losing that, has lost all? Should I point to one of you, and be able by looking down into future years, to say to the rest, your associate here will hereafter be insane, and roam round a wretched maniac, would you not rather weep than laugh? You saw me affected when I began to speak; I will tell you why. I had a friend once; he was dear to me as a brother; he was everything I could wish in a friend. The character of his mind was such as raised in his friends high expectations. I have, indeed, seldom if ever seen his equal. He could grasp any subject, and what others found difficult, only served as amusement for him. I have many of his letters, which would not disgrace any well-educated man, although written by him when he was a school-boy. I expected to see him taking a lead in the affairs of men, and that his opinions would be quoted by others. I saw him after an absence of two years. Where? do you ask. It was in a cage! and even then he was chained! He was a maniac of the most decided character. The moment he saw me, he seized my hand with wild joy, and for a while refused to release it. He had, in his madness, torn the skin from his own, and when I freed myself, my hand was reddened by his blood. For years he has wandered about, when it was safe to liberate him. But he is now and always will be a miserable maniac. I have known sorrow, have seen friends die that were as near as friends could be; but the hour that I sat by the confined and crazy Bernet, *was an hour of the greatest anguish I ever knew.*

"Remember, my pupils, from what has passed this hour, to render unfeigned thanks to God, for continuing your reason hitherto; and if ever again you are disposed to laugh, when a crazy man passes, remember what *may be* your own condition hereafter."

Seize such opportunities, and improve them with a high regard to the best interest of your pupils. In all your intercourse with scholars, it is incumbent on you to make use of every means, not only to promote their present welfare, but to lay the foundation of those habits of thinking and acting which will promote their greatest happiness hereafter. By keeping this constantly in mind, you may be the occasion of lasting benefit to them, and have the satisfaction of reflecting that you have done your duty. If you fail of doing your duty faithfully, conscience will upbraid you, whether patrons do or not.

Allow me to offer a few suggestions, with reference to the best means of exciting a deep interest in the minds of scholars, and leading them to faithful improvement of their time. *Once* there was very little difference in the opinions or practices of instructors with reference to this subject. If any means could be used, " to make children ambitious," it was not a question whether these should be resorted to. In the college, in the academy, in the primary school, *one* was urged to try to excel *another*. Classes in the latter must have a " head," and of course a " foot." Preferments, or " appointments," prizes, medals, in the former, had sufficient power to induce scholars to constant competition.

But there has been a change; many schools are now conducted on principles widely different. An examination of results attendant on the different courses pursued may lead to beneficial conclusions; and having been engaged for many years in conducting the studies of the young, I beg leave to state some of the results I have observed, and the opinions I have formed from these results.

During several of the first years devoted to teaching school, I had recourse to the common means of making scholars " ambitious." Classes in reading, grammar, arithmetic, and geography, as well as spelling, were permitted to have a " head," and to take rank according to their ability to repeat the lesson assigned. I often directed *one* to study his lesson, till able to recite it with as much ease as another had done. I gave tickets and rewards to the successful competitors.

The following were the usual, I may add, the invariable results.

1. A small part of the school applied themselves to their lessons with great earnestness.

2. They aimed to get the lessons for recitation, but thought little of learning them for the purpose of applying knowledge to the practical purposes of life.

3. Efforts were relaxed, whenever the prospect of "beating" became faint."

4. Those near the head were usually jealous of each other, and not unfrequently exhibited envy and ill-will.

5. Those often obtained the prize who were the least deserving of it; for, while one could recite a lesson by an hour's application, and another must devote two or three hours to it, the former was frequently idle a part of the time, and studied less than the latter.

6. Those who had become considerably acquainted with a study, had greatly the advantage of others in their class who had enjoyed less opportunity. Such competitors were, therefore, placed on unequal grounds.

7. Parents were frequently led to take the part of their children, and to believe they were treated unfairly. In this way difficulties originated whi extended through the neighborhood.

After observing such results in different school and different States, I was convinced that this course involved moral evil. This led to an inquiry, whether some other motives might not be presented, which would subserve my purpose better; and the experiment was first made with the same scholars, among whom I had previously attempted to *excite* emulation.

My *first* endeavor was to make the studies more interesting.

2. To show the value of knowledge.

3. To excite a wish to gratify parents and teacher.

4. To show the value of time, the responsibility of scholars to themselves, their parents, and especially to God.

5. I urged them to improve time as a means of securing their own happiness, and a preparation for usefulness in the world.

Among the results immediately witnessed, were the following: —

1. Far better lessons.
2. A much more punctual and regular attendance at school.
3. Much more affection and kindness among the scholars.
4. The scholars were more easily governed.
5. My pleasure in teaching was increased.
6. Parents were pleased, and led to wonder what had taken place at school, which made their children so much more interested in being there.
7. Punishments were almost or entirely unnecessary.

Similar results have been uniform, and very seldom have I found any one who is not pleased with the acquisition of knowledge, and willing to make commendable efforts from that motive simply, in order to obtain it.

In concluding this topic let me say, present to your scholars their obligations to study as a duty, which if properly regarded will add to their happiness, but if disregarded will subject them to the reprehension of their own consciences. It is a duty they owe to themselves. They are under obligation to regard their own happiness, and to make all reasonable preparation for it. They have an opportunity to add to their enjoyment by increasing their knowledge. To disregard it, and to misimprove the opportunity afforded them, will lay the foundation for subsequent sorrow and regret.

It is a duty they owe to their teacher, to make the best use of his instructions. His time is devoted to them. He is anxious to help them, and affords every reasonable assistance in the acquisition of knowledge.

It is a duty they owe to their parents, to make the best improvement of the facilities afforded them for gaining knowledge. They have furnished the means for making improvement in that which will be useful to them in after life, and it is an abuse of parental solicitude and anxiety, not to make all the advances in knowledge of which they are capable.

It is a duty they owe to their country, to qualify themselves to be useful citizens; and this cannot be done, if they remain ignorant and uncultivated. The country has a claim on all to be as useful as they have the means to be; this claim reaches children, as well as those of maturer years.

Lastly, it is a duty they owe him who made them. He requires them to make a due improvement of their time; and promises his favor to those who obey, and threatens his displeasure against those who disregard his command.

"Take fast hold of instruction, let her not go; keep her, for she is thy life. Get wisdom, get understanding, and forget it not. Wisdom is better than rubies, and all the things that may be desired, are not to be compared to it." Such are the declarations of the book of God, and they require serious attention from the youthful scholar.

To conclude: Make use of every proper motive to lead the scholar to just views of the value of knowledge, the best means of gaining and using it when acquired. Point out plainly the consequences which must result to himself and others, from indifference and inattention to the opportunity he has of gaining knowledge.

It is believed that such inducements will be found abundantly sufficient to excite all the attention and application necessary to insure success in acquiring knowledge, except in instances where there is an entire want or perversion of every common principle. There may be instances where everything will fail, except extreme severity. But such are very uncommon, and owe their existence to the neglect or imprudence of parents or teachers. If such instances occur, it may be necessary to resort to unusual means, and these must be left to the judgment of the instructor to apply, as the exigencies of the case may require.

LECTURE XII.

YOUNG LADIES AND GENTLEMEN: —

IN the preceding Lectures, I have discussed most of the topics designed. To all the suggestions made, I trust you have given that attention their importance demands. But, before closing, allow me to call your attention to some additional means of benefiting those who may come under your instruction. These may not be made available in some neighborhoods, or all schools. In many they may be. Indeed, something of the kind can be attempted in most districts, or schools, taught by females as well as males. It is your duty to employ the means already suggested; to adopt the best plans for governing and teaching the youth committed to your care, and equally your duty to resort to other measures, whenever and wherever practicable; by which deeper interest may be awakened in the community, to the appropriate training of the rising generation. The character of the age, and the daily advancements making in your profession particularly, call for something further. Popular education is exciting new interest in the country; and many, who once looked upon themselves as having outlived the time of improvement, are now learning that they may, by efforts easily made, retrieve some of the losses heretofore sustained.

The spirit of improvement ought certainly to be carried into your schools. In accomplishing this, you are to take the lead in the districts to which your labors are devoted. Any school may become a LYCEUM. It may not, indeed, assume all the features of a town or county society, but still be a society for mutual improvement. An easy and certain method may be devised for awakening an interest in every neighborhood.

When we recall to mind the names of a long list of self-taught and self-made men, and examine the results of their efforts and labors, we have the strongest encouragement to direct the attention of those under our influence, to what *they* may achieve. It is unquestionably true that many, who otherwise would be discouraged by the difficulties which they meet, or observe in the prospect before them, may, however, be stimulated and assisted to pursue such a course as will lead them to respectability and usefulness: *this* is to be done by the intellectual discipline and the practical knowledge which they may acquire at the period, and especially by the means within their reach.

But, you will ask, how can this be accomplished? I will suggest some of those means which occur to me as easy and practicable.

In the first place, having succeeded in establishing order in your school, extend an invitation to those scholars who are willing to make uncommon efforts for acquiring knowledge, to meet you on some evening. Say to them, expressly, you wish none to attend but those who are willing to exert themselves to make attainments in useful knowledge, beyond the usual subjects introduced into school. In this way attention will be excited, and you will find but few who will stay away. When you meet them, it may be useful to read or repeat to them the history of some individual, like Franklin or Rittenhouse; or, perhaps, give account of some of the improvements which have been made in facilitating labor or promoting the convenience of man. The wonderful powers of steam, and the uses to which it can be and is applied, in propelling vessels, conducting railroad cars, turning machinery, forging anchors, spinning cotton, printing books, or any of its thousand well-known uses, will be to the point. The object is, to arouse attention and promote thought. If you can excite young persons to *think*, a most important object is gained, and the door is effectually opened for improvement. Till this is done, but little can be accomplished towards benefiting them in any important degree.

After you have gained this point, you may next present some particular subject for an exercise. It may be connected with the studies of the school or business of life. It ought not, however, to interfere with the school exercises, or tend to take off attention from those subjects which are of primary importance. The following outlines of a system upon this subject are offered for the consideration of teachers.

On the first evening, let those who are disposed to attend, be requested to state everything they can concerning the history of the town in which they live; and if any are sufficiently acquainted with drawing, they can give a map of it. As a preparation for this historical exercise, they may be requested to visit and converse with some of those who have been inhabitants of the place for a long period of time. The oldest residents will be able to relate many particulars very interesting to the young. This exercise, attended with suitable remarks from the instructor, will be both pleasant and useful to the school, and others who attend. It would certainly add to the interest of the exercise on the part of the pupils, if an intelligent citizen, well acquainted with the history of the town or neighborhood, should attend and relate the most important facts with which he is familiar.

Then let one be requested to write an account of some interesting historical event, such as the discovery of this country, the battles of Lexington, Bunker Hill, Bennington, Saratoga, etc. To a second may be assigned some other historical subject. It will be necessary to assign exercises sufficient to occupy the evening. Another evening, let each one be requested to give, as far as proper, an account of the business in which he, or the family to which he belongs, may be engaged; stating its profits, and its difficulties or facilities. A third evening may be devoted to rhetorical exercises; and another, to free remarks on some important question. Another may be spent in reading interesting accounts of some parts of our own country, or of some other part of the world, time being allowed for making remarks on the subjects. Let an evening be assigned also for the purpose of answering questions proposed to you by the pupils.

It will not be necessary to have these exercises confined to males. The females have often more knowledge, and are better scholars, than any of the young men found in a district. In all cases, where practicable, females should be urged to take a part in the School-Lyceum, and to be present at the meetings.

It will be useful to them and interesting to others, to give some account of housewifery. A description of the process of making cheese, an account of the best mode of making butter, or even of the manner of making a loaf of bread, or brewing beer, would be heard with pleasure, and not without advantage, in almost any place. Domestic economy generally, is a proper subject of attention, and one on which they may, with the utmost propriety, be requested to read compositions. Many other exercises will claim the attention of females, as much as that of young men. All the subjects which I shall hereafter mention are of this class.

I have been the more particular in these remarks, from the fact that sufficient attention is not usually paid to female improvement.

After proper attention has been given to the exercises already mentioned, and others of the same kind, you can proceed to introduce some of the more important principles of natural philosophy, and chemistry, with simple experiments. Moral philosophy claims particular attention. The younger members may, at the same time, have lessons in geometry, and its applications to the business and purposes of life. "Holbrook's First Lessons," accompanied with a card of diagrams, will afford great amusement, and be highly profitable to scholars of eight or ten years of age. By the same class, the "Little Philosopher; or, Infant School at Home," might be used with great advantage. It is an admirable work.

When sufficient attention has been given to such studies, the way will be prepared for the regular formation of a lyceum, on the general principles of these institutions. The importance of apparatus will now be perceived. You will, of course, make it a subject of early attention. To obtain this will be an object of high importance, as it will be a means of facilitating the operations of the lyceum, and will make it a common property.

Another means of increasing the interest felt by your scholars in these subjects, will be to give or engage others to give familiar lectures, furnishing food for reflection, and throwing light on the subjects of study connected with the business and the wants of life. Is there a physician in your vicinity? engage him to give some familiar lectures on the human system, the means of preserving health, or some other theme within the range of his profession. Is there a lawyer? he may point out the several principles of the common law; the distinction between this and statute law; the necessity to every citizen of a certain amount of legal knowledge, etc. Is there an ingenious mechanic? he may tell something about the nature, importance, and uses of his trade. The minister may be requested to give a lecture on the importance of moral philosophy, or he may explain the nature of the Christian religion, the value and influence of the Bible, etc. etc. By thus engaging foreign assistance, you will be conferring a double benefit. First, the instruction given will be important and highly useful of itself; and secondly, by engaging the attention of those who take a lead in society, you will render the lyceum popular.

You may also confer an important benefit on the neighborhood in which you are employed, by promoting the formation of a library of scientific and useful books. The attention of the young is not sufficiently given to reading of the most *useful* kind. Young persons are generally better pleased with works of fiction, than with those best calculated to discipline their minds, and to cultivate a good taste. The prevalent taste for reading is, in a degree, vitiated; and whoever is instrumental of correcting it, in a single neighborhood, will unquestionably be a public benefactor. The proportion of *light* reading, which has been patronized for a few years past, is altogether too large. The "Annuals," "Albums," novels, etc, etc. which have recently been eagerly sought after and read, are exerting a ruinous influence, especially by becoming the occasion of corrupting the taste, and leading the young to neglect those books which would be highly beneficial. I cannot but urge it, therefore, as highly important, that you exert an influence in favor of a more useful kind of reading. Whenever you can direct the attention of your scholars to those books which will lead to a habit of close thinking, you will deserve the thanks of every friend to the young. I am fully persuaded, that neither parents nor instructors are sufficiently awake to the effects of the prevalent light reading of the present day. Nothing is accounted interesting, to a class of readers, but that which abounds with *incident*, *adventure*, *and catastrophe.* A love-tale, or something of similar character, is woven into almost everything written for the young, and has charms for many, (must I say for some professedly pious youth ?) greater than a book of travels, voyages, history, or geography. To such, a scientific book has ordinarily few charms. Is there not danger on the whole, that what has been gained on the score of a better mode of teaching, is in danger of being counterbalanced and lost by an injudicious course of reading ? Is there not room to fear, that a desire to *please* the young, has overbalanced a desire to *instruct* them ? If my fears are well founded, you will confer a great benefit on those whom you can persuade to provide, and read attentively, books calculated to promote a knowledge and excite a love of the sciences.

It is my purpose, at this time, to make suggestions only; your own reflections will furnish you with many things connected with the subjects on which I have spoken. Let it be an object with you to adapt your mode of operations to the exigences of your situation. I am aware, that the directions which I have given cannot be followed in all cases. If a lyceum already exists, or if a course of exercises has been marked out, you will need to pursue that mode which will have the best effect, considered with reference to existing circumstances. In some cases, it may be impracticable to attempt anything more than to call your scholars together, and instruct them in geometry, by the help of the First Lessons and cards before mentioned. But, by all means, do *something* towards effecting the objects contemplated by lyceums. All of you *may* do something, and must be governed by circumstances as to the best mode. Let not the season pass, however, without making the attempt. Absolute failure, on your part, is preferable to inactivity. Should you not succeed, you will have the pleasure, at least, of reflecting that you have tried to benefit the members who compose your important charge. It will certainly be in your power to disseminate some important intelligence on the subject of popular education. The seed thus sown, may spring up hereafter, under the influence of a warmer sun. Discouragement is not to be indulged, till your efforts have absolutely failed; and if you go forward with your work steadily, manfully, and perseveringly, you may be assured that they will not fail.

Permit me to say, in the conclusion of this Lecture, that much will depend on the impression you make on the parents of your scholars. If you can interest them, there will be but little doubt of your success in interesting their children. Be careful, then, to have your objects thoroughly understood by them in the first place. A demand on their purses would be improper, till you have convinced them both that they ought to do something more to benefit their scholars, and also how this may be effected.

Having once convinced them of the utility of apparatus, the means for procuring it will generally be obtained without great difficulty. Let the scholars themselves become the advocates for appropriations. Some encouragement from yourself, will afterwards be necessary; and, in a majority of cases, I have no doubt it will be attended with success. If parents are parsimonious here, their unreasonableness ought to be fully shown. It is certainly true that parsimony is frequently bad economy; and it may be made to appear so. A few dollars expended for apparatus or judicious books, may prevent the young from forming a habit of seeking amusement in a more expensive manner. In a word, satisfy parents what is their true interest, in regard to their children, and your work is accomplished.

Yield to no discouragements which you may encounter. The object you have in view, is too important to be abandoned in consequence of small obstacles. Remember the maxim, " Labor conquers all things." If success does not attend your first efforts, let it be a stimulus to greater exertion, rather than a reason for discouragement. Resolve to succeed, and maintain your determination; if your efforts are discreetly directed, some success will inevitably follow. The interest thus awakened in a single winter has been followed by very cheering results.

www.ingramcontent.com/pod-product-compliance
Lightning Source LLC
La Vergne TN
LVHW050527100826
845148LV00002B/464

* 9 7 8 1 4 2 5 5 1 9 7 9 7 *